RANDOM SELECTIONS

By

Cecelia Frances Page

iUniverse, Inc.
New York   Bloomington

Random Selections

iUniverse books may be ordered through booksellers or by contacting:

iUniverse
1663 Liberty Drive
Bloomington, IN 47403
www.iuniverse.com
1-800-Authors (1-800-288-4677)

Because of the dynamic nature of the Internet, any Web addresses or links contained in this book may have changed since publication and may no longer be valid.

ISBN: 978-1-4502-0224-4 (sc)
ISBN: 978-1-4502-0225-1 (ebk)

Printed in the United States of America

iUniverse rev. date: 1/14/2010

CONTENTS

PREFACE

RANDOM SELECTIONS

RANDOM SELECTIONS is an exciting book of 60 stories and articles with a wide variety of topics. FANTASY STORIES are The Deep Blue Sea, The Leprechaun Kingdom and The Enchanting Garden. TRAVEL TOPICS are Ships At Sea, Life in New Zealand, Summer Cruise, Life in Israel, Jungle Adventures and Learn About Central America. PHILOSOPHICAL TOPICS are Heavenly Realms, Higher Consciousness, Worthwhile Endeavors, Seeking Truth, Existentialism, Healing Consciousness, Daily Prayers and Self Realization.

SCIENCE TOPICS are Our World Is Changing, Birds Around the World, Overcoming Diseases and Astronauts Go to the Moon. HUMAN INTEREST TOPICS are The Way We Were, High Chair Experiences, Appearances, Why People Shave, The Scholar, Puzzlements and Predicaments and Keeping Secrets, Betty Hutton's Life, Private Lives Of Movie Stars. ADVENTURE TOPICS are Magnificent Times,

Sky Maser's Victory, Unusual Experiences, Weekend Adventures, Beach Adventures and Jungle Adventures. EDUCATIONAL TOPICS are Marie Montessori's Educational System, Experiences During School Days, The Scholar, Learning to Read, Educated People, Learning Foreign Languages, Use Your Imagination, Gaining and Losing Weight, Facts About America and Teaching Piano. POLITICAL TOPICS are Presidential Secrets, Upholding Freedom, Dictatorships That Fell and Why Certain People Become Radicals. OTHER TOPICS are Our World Is Changing, Why Certain Stores Succeed, Atlantean Mysteries, Playing Tennis, Becoming Self Published, Household Figurines, Temple Conventions and New Generations Bring Changes.

RANDOM SELECTIONS includes both fiction and nonfiction stories and articles.

ABOUT THE AUTHOR

Cecelia Frances Page has published five, original screenplays and three, original, poetry books. Her original screenplays are entitled *WALKING IN THE LIGHT, FLASHBACKS, CELESTIAL CONNECTIONS I AND II* and *ADVENTURES IN LEMURIA I AND II*. Her three, original, poetry books are *COSMIC DIMENSIONS, VIVID IMPRESSIONS* and *SIGNIFICANT INTROSPECTIONS*. Cecelia Frances Page has written over five hundred, original poems. Several of her poems are published in *THE WORLD'S BEST POEMS OF 2004 AND 2005*.

Cecelia has been writing poems since the age of 19. She has written 50 books. Some of her books published by iUniverse Publishers are *Westward Pursuit, Opportune Times, Imagine If, Fortunately, Mystical Realities, Magnificent Celestial Journeys, Extraordinary Encounters, Brilliant Candor, Expand Your Awareness, Seek Enlightenment Within, Vivid Memories of Halcyon, Awaken to Spiritual Illumination, Adventures on Ancient Continents, Pathways to Spiritual Realization, Celestial*

Connections, Phenomenal Experiences, Celestial Beings From Outer Space, Awesome Episodes, Incredible Times, Interpretations of Life, New Perspectives, Tremendous Moments, Amazing Stories and Articles, Horizons Beyond, Fascinating Topics, Adventurous Experiences, Certain People Make A Difference, Tangible Realities, Relevant Interests, Power of Creative and Worthwhile Living, Extraterrestrial Civilizations on Earth, The Future Age Beyond The New Age Movement, Remarkable World Travels, Impressionable Occurrences, Immense Possibilities, Significant Moments, Random Selections and more.

Cecelia Frances Page has a B.A. and M.A. in Education with a focus in English, Speech, Drama, Music and Psychology. Cecelia is an excellent pianist and vocal soloist. She teaches piano and voice as a music teacher. She is an author, educator, drama director, philosopher, photographer and artist. She is an elementary school teacher as well. Cecelia believes that creative abilities and talents can be achieved. Cecelia Frances Page continues to write more worthwhile books to inspire her readers.

ONE

THE WAY WE WERE

Lucille Jones was an intelligent, well educated woman. She was 27 years old and had completed college. She earned a college degree in Interior Decorating. She was working as an interior decorator around the city of New York City.

Lucille Jones had an opportunity to meet different clients who wanted their homes decorated. She answered the phone at an interior decorator's office. She wrote down the names, phone numbers and addresses of different clients. Lucille set up appointments for different clients.

Lucille drove her car to each client she was assigned to so she could see their home before redecorating them. She drove to the Albertsons to look at their house in Manhattan. Mrs. Albertson greeted Lucille at the door. Mrs. Albertson said, "Hello. Are you Lucille Jones?" Lucille replied, "Yes. I have come to look at your house so that I can redecorate it." Mrs. Anderson responded, "Please come in. I have been expecting you." Lucille walked into Mrs. Anderson's house. She began looking around to evaluate the house.

Mrs. Anderson said, "Will you be able to make the house more modern with bright colors?" Lucille noticed the walls were a muggy brown with uncolorful designs which were unattractive. The house looked dark and old fashioned. Lucille thought about what colors would make the house look modern and attractive. Lucille said, "I think bright yellow walls and a cheerful lavender trim around the wood panels would look good in the living room and lounge room. Would you like this color scheme?"

Mrs. Anderson, known as Alice, replied, "These colors are attractive. Use these colors. You can call me Alice." Lucille looked at the kitchen. She noticed it looked a dingy, dark orange with brown paneling. Lucille remarked, "Your kitchen will look cheerful if it is painted bright yellow with bright orange paneling. The floor would look good with bright mosaic designs of yellow, white and orange. The kitchen curtains should be white to match the new décor." Alice responded, "I like your ideas. What about the bathrooms? What colors do you suggest?"

Lucille looked at the two bathrooms. They both looked dingy gray and black. Lucille suggested, "The bathrooms could be pastel pink and yellow walls with bright mosaic shower walls. The floors can be pastel lavender. Brightly designed shower curtains will add to the décor. Shell shaped sinks will look exotic in the bathrooms." Alice replied, "It sounds good. Go ahead and use all your plans."

Lucille said, "I need to see the bedroom next." Alice showed Lucille the master bedroom first. Lucille noticed this bedroom was cluttered. Colorful wallpaper can be rolled on parts of each wall to add to the décor. Blending curtains with orange, white and yellow designs will affect the walls. The floor can be recovered with a soft, beige carpet to blend with the bedroom. The king-size bed can be moved closer to the window. This will give you more room to walk around. The dressers can be moved closer together to make even more room for other furniture. The heaps of newspapers and miscellaneous things can be stored in new shelves which I can purchase. Your bedroom will no longer look cluttered and drab."

Alice looked interested in Lucille's suggestions. She said, "Thanks for your ideas. When can you start redecorating my house?" Lucille remarked, "I can start next Monday. I still am busy decorating another house." Alice replied, "Fine. You can start next Monday. Thanks for coming to look at my house. I look forward to the new changes."

Lucille left Alice Albertson's house. It was midday. She decided to eat lunch at a Deli Diner several blocks away. She ordered a tuna sandwich on toasted rye bread with mustard, dark green lettuce, watercress, sliced tomatoes, sliced avocado and sliced onions. Large tooth-picks were pierced through the cut sandwich. Lucille had creole vegetable soup and potato salad with this lunch meal. She also drank mango ice tea. When she was done eating her lunch she felt very full.

After lunch Lucille got back in her car. She drove to her next assignment in Brooklyn. She met a single man who was 37. He was tall, attractive with black hair and brown eyes. His name was Jeff Letterman. Jeff greet-ed Lucille at his deluxe townhouse. She walked in and looked around. She encountered an uncreative décor with very little blending, color schemes. His townhouse was gray and black and some walls were white. Lucille suggested flamboyant colors such as a cheerful salmon, coral and off-tones of gold and red on the walls. The panels would look good painted a bright magenta col-or. Lucille suggested yellow-beige carpets in the living room, dining room, hallways and bedrooms. The bed-rooms would look good painted with light turquoise paneling with exotic wallpaper which blended with the paneling.

Jeff noticed that Lucille was young, attractive and capable as an interior decorator. Lucille had red hair, blue eyes and a slender figure. She was dressed in a pur-ple pant suit. She wore a gold scarf around her neck with gold shoes to match her outfit. Lucille wore a styl-ish, short hairdo. Her red hair stood out and she looked stunning. Her teeth were sparkling white. Her blue eyes sparkled and twinkled when she smiled. Jeff was attracted to Lucille. He listened attentively when she spoke to him about his townhouse. She clarified a number of positive suggestions to improve the appearance of his townhouse. Jeff told Lucille to decorate it the way she thought his townhouse should look.

Lucille told Jeff she would be back in several days to work on the colors around Jeff's townhouse. She said goodbye and left. It was time to go home. Lucille drove to her apartment near Central Park. She drove into her driveway and opened the apartment garage. She parked her car in her garage. Lucille went into her one bedroom apartment.

It was approximately 6:15 p.m. on Thursday night. Lucille had been busy all day. She was tired and needed to rest. Lucille turned on soft, relaxing music to listen to while she got into her night clothes. She selected a TV chicken dinner with mashed potatoes, string beans and berry pie and warmed this TV dinner up in the oven for 45 minutes. She prepared some hot, herb mint tea to sip while she relaxed in her comfortable, recliner chair.

Lucille thought about her different, interior, decorating assignments. She hoped to complete each assignment on time and to please each customer. She hoped to receive more customers once her present assignments were finished.

Suddenly, the phone rang in Lucille's apartment. She answered her phone. She said, "Hello." Jeff responded,

"Hi, Lucille. I'm calling to ask you out." Lucille reacted, "Are you asking me for a date?" Jeff answered, "Yes. I would like to become more acquainted with you." Lucille replied, "I don't mix pleasure with business." Jeff felt disappointed. But he didn't give up. He said over his cell phone, "I hope you change your mind. I won't bite!"

Lucille felt uncomfortable. Her company's policy was that employees were not allowed to date customers. So, Lucille replied, "It is my company's policy that I cannot date customers. I'm sorry. I can't go out with you." Jeff responded, "Perhaps, when you have completed your interior decorating in my townhouse you will be able to go on dates with me." Lucille answered, "I will consider dating you when you are no longer a customer. I will be over to work on your townhouse tomorrow. Goodbye." Lucille hung up. She felt concerned that she had to tell Jeff that she couldn't date him when he was no longer a customer. She didn't want to lose her job.

Lucille took her TV dinner out of the oven. She unwrapped the foil and let it cool for five minutes. She poured more herb mint tea. She sat down near a small table in her living room to eat her TV dinner while she watched the news on television. She listened to what was happening in the world. She tried to relax while she ate her dinner. She thought about Jeff. She was attracted to him. She wanted to go on dates with Jeff. She would have to wait until her interior decorating assignment was over before she could date him.

The next day Lucille drove over to Jeff's townhouse. She brought painters to paint each room according to her directions. The new paints had been mixed to be used. The painters spent several days painting all the rooms. Furniture had been rearranged in the living room and lounge room. More space was created in the bedrooms. New, blending curtains were ordered. Once they arrived the new curtains were put on curtain rods over the windows around the townhouse.

Within two weeks Jeff's townhouse had been redecorated according to Lucille's plan. Jeff observed the new décor in his townhouse. He was pleased with the changes that Lucille had made in the townhouse. Lucille Jones had completed her work assignment at Jeff Letterman's townhouse in Brooklyn. Jeff decided to ask Lucille for a date now that she wasn't working for him anymore. She was still at his townhouse on the last day of her assignment there. Jeff stood near Lucille. He said, "Please go out with me tomorrow night for dinner." Lucille looked at Jeff warmly. She replied, "Alright. What time should I be ready?" Jeff looked excited and he replied, "Be ready at 7 p.m." Lucille replied, "I'll be ready. Should I dress up?" Jeff answered, "I'm taking you to a classy restaurant."

Lucille decided to dress up. She selected a beautiful pastel, lavender dress with lace sleeves and rimming around the top of the silk dress. She wore gold colored earrings and a gold necklace and attractive gold shoes with her silk, lavender dress. She looked magnificent in this dress. She curled her hair and created a glamorous hairstyle to look even more attractive. She was dazzling to look at all dressed up with a fancy hairstyle.

Jeff arrived at Lucille's apartment at 7 p.m. the next night. He rang the doorbell. Lucille came to the door to greet him. Jeff noticed how glamorous Lucille was. He smiled and said, "Hi. You look great!" Lucille smiled and said, "Thank you." Jeff was dressed in an attractive blue sports jacket and matching beige pants. He wore a yellow shirt and black leather shoes. He was wearing a red tie. His hair was neatly combed. He looked distinguished.

Jeff escorted Lucille to his four door, green Nissan. He opened the front passenger door. Lucille sat in the front passenger seat. Jeff walked over to the driver's side and got in. Jeff drove across town to Greenwich Village to an exotic Mediterranean restaurant. He opened the door for Lucille. She stepped out of the car. Jeff and Lucille walked into the Mediterranean restaurant. This exotic restaurant was decorated with European paintings and artifacts such as colorful vases, statuettes and European handicrafts such as a variety of pottery. A waterfall flowed down a rock formation into a miniature pool. Potted plants were arranged around this restaurant.

A host, dressed in a black suit and bow tie and white shirt, escorted Jeff and Lucille to a corner table near the waterfall and pond. He handed them fancy menus once they were seated. Jeff and Lucille studied the menus. A server dressed in a black suit, white shirt and black bow tie, came to their table with water, bread and butter. The server asked what Jeff and Lucille would like to order for dinner. Jeff was familiar with this restaurant. He ordered Bass, a delicate sautéed fish with wild rice and a medley of steamed, seasoned vegetables. Lucille wasn't sure what to order. Jeff recommended lobster and shrimp. So, Lucille ordered lobster and shrimp with scalloped potatoes covered with a creamy sauce and a medley of steamed, seasoned vegetables. Jeff ordered white wine. Green salads were served with this order as well.

Lucille sipped some water. She selected a piece of sourdough bread. She spread butter on her bread. Jeff and Lucille listened to soft classical music while they ate their bread. They enjoyed looking at the picturesque waterfall and pond.

The server brought white wine to Jeff and Lucille's table. He carefully opened the wine bottle. He poured white wine into two wine glasses. Jeff lifted his wine glass. He spoke to Lucille. He said, "Here is a salute to our first date together." Lucille lifted her wine glass. Jeff tapped his wine glass on Lucille's wine glass. They sipped their wine slow Jeff looked very warmly at Lucille. He said, "I'm glad we finally are dating." Lucille smiled at

Jeff. She remained silent. Jeff continued, "This is one of the best restaurants in New York City. I hope you like it." Lucille smiled again. She decided to respond. She replied, "This is a beautiful restaurant. I have never been here before. The waterfall is magnificent overlooking the pond." Jeff remarked, "This is my favorite restaurant. This is why I brought you here."

The server brought two green salads to Jeff and Lucille and placed a salad before each of them. The server asked if they wanted some pepper put on their salads. Jeff accepted some pepper. Lucille said she didn't want any pepper. They began eating their salads which had a Mediterranean salad dressing on them.

While they ate Jeff talked about himself. He spoke about his childhood and school background. Lucille found out that Jeff grew up in Milwaukee, Illinois where the famous pianist, Liberace, grew up. Jeff said he began playing the piano when he was 7 years old. Jeff could play a variety of piano pieces. He played classical jazz, Broadway and Swing piano pieces. He also learned to sing vocal solos. He sang popular songs as well as classical, vocal solos.

Lucille was curious about Jeff's musical abilities and accomplishments. She hoped to hear him sing and play the piano. Lucille said, "I would like to hear you sing and play the piano." Jeff replied, "I have a grand piano in my townhouse. I will perform for you whenever you like." Lucille's eyes lit up as she looked intently and warmly at Jeff. She continued to eat her green salad.

The server brought the main course to Jeff and Lucille's table. He carefully placed the lobster and shrimp dinner in front of Lucille. He then placed the bass (fish) in front of Jeff. The food looked sumptuous. Lucille and Jeff began eating their main course. Lucille poured a lobster sauce over her lobster. Both the lobster and the shrimp were cooked to perfection. The medley of seasoned, steamed vegetables were very fresh and tasty.

For dessert Jeff and Lucille selected from a large silver tray of pastries. Lucille selected a custard-filled pastry. Jeff selected a chocolate éclair. All the desserts looked very appetizing. They enjoyed their scrumptious desserts while they listened to classical, background music.

After dinner Jeff took Lucille for a drive around New York City to observe the city lights. Then he took her to a nightclub called the Copacabana for a night cap. They sat at a table overlooking New York Harbor. They saw lit up ships in the harbor. The moon gleamed over the ocean. This scenic view was a romantic setting.

Jeff asked Lucille to dance while they were at the nightclub. He held her gently while they danced over and over. He continued to hold her closely in a romantic manner. Lucille didn't resist Jeff's close embraces.

She was happy to be with him and she was having a wonderful time.

Jeff continued to ask Lucille out for dates. He took her out to different restaurants and nightclubs in New York City. They strolled through Central Park to enjoy the scenic view. They took a harbor cruise to see the New York coastline. Jeff took Lucille to several art galleries and museums in New York City. They spent a lot of time together.

Lucille came over to Jeff's townhouse to listen to him sing and play piano solos on his grand piano. Jeff sang "Strangers in Paradise", "Autumn Leaves", "Over the Rainbow" and "Younger Than Springtime." Jeff had a powerful voice. He sang with vocal quality and feeling. Lucille was very impressed the way he sang and played the piano. She realized that Jeff was more talented than she had previously expected.

Jeff dated Lucille for several years. They became very close. In fact, they fell in love. Their love was true love because they began as friends. They shared common interests such as reading, appreciation of music, playing tennis and attending a variety of cultural activities and events.

One day Jeff took Lucille to Central Park. He sat on a bench near her. He took out an engagement ring. He looked at Lucille warmly and asked, "Will you marry me?" Lucille's eyes lit up. She smiled warmly and replied, "Yes." Jeff was overjoyed because he loved Lucille very much. Lucille was very happy. Jeff had finally asked her to marry him.

—— TWO ——

THE DEEP BLUE SEA

In the deep blue sea are many sea life creatures, coral reefs and sea plants. Myths about mermaids and mermen describe how half human and half fish beings lived in the ocean. These mermaids and mermen swam across the sea and explored many underwater caves and coral gardens. They ate sea plants and small fish to survive.

Ola was a young mermaid who swam daily in the deep blue sea with other mermaids. Era, Mala and Roma were other, companion mermaids who swam around with Ola. Ola followed these mermaids into hidden, underwater caves where they played during the day and even slept during the night.

Often, Ola laid on rocks that rose above the sea. Ola sunned herself on rocks when the sun came out. She enjoyed watching beautiful sunrises. She was fascinated with bright colors of yellow, orange and pink in the sky near the horizon which continued to move higher in the sky.

Ola had long, blonde hair and clear, blue eyes. She had white, smooth skin. Her long, blonde hair flowed over her breast. She had a long, scaly fish tail. She was able to stay deep in the deep, blue sea whenever she wanted to. Ola liked to play with sea turtles. She held on to giant turtles one by one and traveled with them for many miles across the sea floor. Ola became acquainted with the giant turtles while she held onto them.

Mio, a male, giant turtle, responded to Ola holding onto his tortoise shell. Ola sang to Mio as they traveled together across the sea. Ola sang a sea song about the currents and ripples of the sea. She sang about the schools of fish who swam by. She sang about the coral beds and sea urchins along the sea floor. Sea anemones moved about hidden in the sea underwater rocks.

As time passed Ola continued to swim in the sea. She discovered some tropical islands in the South Pacific as she swam south. She waddled onto the beach to enjoy seashells lying in the sand. She found a nautilus shell and conch shell in the pristine sand. She touched these shells and was curious why they were there.

On a remote, tropical island in the South Pacific, Ola and her mermaid companions, Era, Mala and Roma frolicked and played among the palm trees. They played with coconuts. They threw coconuts back and forth to each other like regular balls. They laid down against the trunks of palm trees. They ate bananas and berries which they found in the jungle. They were cheerful and happy.

Then, one day as they were playing on the beach of a tropical island, Ola and her mermaid companions heard a peculiar, loud sound. It sounded like thunder roaring in the distance. Ola and her mermaid friends wondered who was making this sound. They became curious. They were unable to travel through the dense, tropical jungle because they could only waddle since they were half fishes with tails.

Yet, Ola and her mermaid companions remained on the pristine beach hoping to find out what was causing the loud sound. Then, suddenly some brown skinned natives appeared on the beach. They were beating drums very loudly as they assembled on the beach.

Ola and her mermaid companions Era, Mala and Roma became frightened. They rushed into the ocean to flee from these natives who were beating drums so loudly. They disappeared beneath the rolling, crashing waves deep in the sea. The natives ran after them. However, the natives were unable to swim too far out to sea.

Ola, Era, Mala and Roma were able to escape these strange, unfamiliar natives. When Ola was far enough away in the ocean she looked back at the natives who attempted to capture her. She was glad she had a long, fish tail so she could swim quickly away. She continued to live in the deep, blue sea with her mermaid companions.

Ola swam around and encountered a group of dolphins moving across the upper currents of the sea. She spoke to the dolphins. They spoke back to Ola as they swam by. Ola got on top of a dolphin and held on to its back and fins. The dolphin accepted Ola and it traveled a long distance in the sea with Ola. She saw many new underwater plants, caves and corals. She heard the sounds of whales calling across the sea.

Ola swam around in the new underwater domains. She missed her mermaid companions. So, she asked the dolphin to take her back to them. The dolphin obeyed her command. Ola was taken back to the mermaids and the mermen underwater caves. Ola was greeted by Era, Mala, Roma and many other mermaids and mermen. She was happy to come home again in the deep, blue sea.

—— THREE ——

THE LEPRECHAUN KINGDOM

In a rich verdant green valley a leprechaun kingdom existed in a pleasant, ideal location away from busy, noisy cities. This leprechaun kingdom was magical with magnificent green trees, bushes and scrubs with an abundant array of wild lupins, poppies, thistle flowers and mustard seed flowers which spread across this leprechaun valley.

A kingdom of leprechauns lived in this leprechaun valley. They dressed in green outfits and wore leprechaun hats and shoes. The leprechaun kingdom lived inside hollow, tree trunks. Thousands of leprechauns lived in a large, pine forest. Leprechaun families lived in specific hollow trees. They shared food which they grew in the leprechauns' valley. Fruit trees and a variety of vegetables were grown. The leprechauns were vegetarians. They were peaceful and lived in harmony in their kingdom. They lived for many centuries in peace and safety.

Then one day large, human intruders came into the leprechaun valley. These large, giant-sized human beings took over this beautiful, peaceful valley. The leprechauns hid in the hollow, tree trunks. When the large intruders walked by their forest homes the leprechauns remained very quiet. They could not be seen in their hollow, tree trunk homes.

The intruders began to cut pine trees down to build new homes to live in. The leprechauns had to move quickly out of trees that were being cut down. Some of the human giants saw the leprechauns come out of hollow tree trunks. They tried to capture these leprechauns. The leprechauns ran away as fast as they could.

However, some of the human intruders grabbed some of the leprechauns with their giant hands. These leprechauns were put in miniature cages and kept as prisoners. They had lost their freedom. The leprechauns were very frustrated and unhappy. They were no longer feeling peaceful.

The leprechauns who escaped from the human giants went further into the forest to resettle in new, hollow tree trunks. They lived in fear of being captured by the giant, human beings. They hoped their new homes would not be cut down. They had to survive on forest plants, nuts, berries and roots to live. Their food supply was more limited now that they were forced to hide constantly from the intruders.

Leaders of the leprechauns decided to find a way to free the leprechauns who had been captured in cages by the giant intruders. They brought knives. A group of leprechauns decided to sneak over to free leprechauns in cages. They traveled by foot at night time so they wouldn't be easily seen. They came over to the cages to free the imprisoned leprechauns.

The imprisoned leprechauns were glad that their comrades had come to free them. Leprechauns began using their small knives to cut the cages made of en-twined ropes. At least one hundred leprechauns began cutting the large, thick entwined ropes. It took hours to cut through the thick ropes.

The human intruders were asleep because it was late at night. There were no human guards observing the cages which were outside on the ground near the pine forest. So, the free leprechauns continued to cut the en-twined ropes to free the imprisoned leprechauns. Finally, some of the entwined ropes were being cut loose. When enough rope was cut the cages fell apart.

The imprisoned leprechauns were freed at last. They rushed out of the broken cages. There were over 200 freed leprechauns. All of the leprechauns rushed away together into the pine forest. They all went back to the trees farther away and continued to live in hollow, tree trunks. They continued to gather food in the forest to survive. They were not able to go back freely into the leprechaun valley during the daytime.

The leprechauns came out very late at night to gather fruit and vegetables from their gardens. However, the intruders began to build more houses where the leprechauns had planted gardens. They were no longer able to gather fruit and vegetables in the leprechaun valley.

Thousands of leprechauns finally moved away from the pine forest. They traveled many miles away to another forest close to a mountain in a remote region. They regretted having to leave their leprechaun kingdom.

——— FOUR ———

MAGNIFICENT TIMES

Many people look forward to magnificent times. Vacations and sudden adventures are exciting and worthwhile. Attending special events and activities are marvelous times to look forward to. People enjoy having a wonderful time lounging, hiking, exploring and doing many different things independently and in groups.

Holly and Gerard Stevenson had just got married. They planned a special honeymoon in the North Pacific in Hawaii and South Pacific in Samoa. They prepared for this magnificent time together. After their wedding and wedding reception they packed their get away car for their special journey.

The newlyweds purchased tickets at the Los Angeles Airport. They drove to the L.A. International Airport to take a flight to Hawaii. The flight to Hawaii took approximately six hours from the Los Angeles airport. During the flight Holly and Gerard sat close together in first class. They were served champagne and delicious appetizers. An evening meal of prime ribs, baby potatoes, asparagus with a creamy cheese sauce and green salad were served. Later, for dessert Holly and Gerard had custard with whipped cream. They were served hot coffee.

Holly and Gerald snuggled close together. They watched a gorgeous, bright sunset from their airplane window. Then they laid back in their recliner seats to rest after viewing the sunset. They listened to relaxing music before falling asleep.

Early the next morning the airplane landed in the Hawaiian airport in Honolulu. Gerard and Holly left the airplane and picked up their luggage at the arrivals section. They rented a taxi at the airport. Gerald asked the taxi driver to take them to the deluxe, Flamingo Pink Hotel in Waikiki. Gerald had reserved a large, wedding suite overlooking Honolulu Harbor. A porter took the Stevensons' luggage to the wedding suite.

Holly and Gerald walked into the attractive lobby and into an elevator on the third floor. Holly and Gerald stepped out of the elevator. They walked to their wedding suite. Gerald unlocked the door. Then he carried Holly over the threshold into the hotel suite. Holly and Gerald enjoyed the magnificent view of the Honolulu Harbor. There were flower arrangements in the suite.

There were orchids, hibiscus and lilies arranged in a large vase. The suite smelled clean and fragrant. The suite was elegant and spacious. Holly and Gerard were alone together at last. They were able to become intimate in the privacy of their hotel suite. Gerald was attentive and passionate to Holly.

The next morning after a delicious breakfast Gerald, and Holly dressed in bathing suits and brought beach towels with them. They walked on Waikiki Beach. They walked into the ocean and felt waves crashing down on them. They began swimming in the ocean. They saw tourists in rowboats and kayaks. Larger ships were anchored in the distance. The ocean was a beautiful turquoise- blue. It was a heavenly, clear day.

Holly and Gerard browsed around at the International Market downtown. They went into a number of exotic shops. Later, they went to a luau on Waikiki Beach. Roast pork, poi, fresh cut fruit, rice and cut vegetables plus bread and butter were served at large tables to at least 75 tourists. Hawaiian dancers dressed in Hawaiian costumes performed Hawaiian dances. A fire performer put fire in his mouth. Tourists were taught Hawaiian dances after dinner. The sunset over the horizon was very magnificent. Many bright color hues emerged in the sky.

Holly and Gerard took a rented car up to Diamond Point near Waikiki. They witnessed glittering rocks which appeared to look like sparkling diamonds. They found out the glittering stones were not really diamonds. They were able to gaze at a panoramic view of Waikiki and Honolulu Harbor.

Later, Gerard and Holly decided to drive along the coast to the Polynesian Cultural Center. The view of the coastline and ocean were spectacular. Different beaches were visible along their trip. The Polynesian Cultural Center was an exciting place to enjoy six Polynesian cultures. Gerard and Holly watched Polynesians climb palm trees to collect coconuts. They watched Polynesians prepare shredded coconut. They chopped coconuts in half to drink coconut juice.

A Polynesian Show was presented in late afternoon. Many cultural dances were performed by different Polynesians such as Hawaiians, Tahitians, Samoans, Fijians, Maoris and Tongans. They wore their traditional, Polynesian costumes. Many of them wore large, head dresses with many bright colors. Special lighting added color and mystery to the stage. Polynesian music was played with guitars, ukuleles and drums. The Polynesian show was enchanting. Holly and Gerard enjoyed this show immensely.

The next morning Holly and Gerard flew to Kauai. The plane flew over the Grand Canyon of Kauai which is like a miniature Grand Canyon in Arizona. White eagles were hovering in this magnificent canyon. Rich, red soil was in layers with scrubs and tropical trees along the canyon floor. Holly and Gerard looked out of the window of the airplane to enjoy the spectacular view of the Grand Canyon of Kauai, which is the second largest canyon in the world.

When the plane landed Holly and Gerard rented a car at the Kauai Airport. They drove along the main road until they came to a large hotel. They had booked in advance to stay at the Kauai Hotel. Once their luggage was placed in their hotel suite they changed clothes and went walking on the pristine beach. There were conch shells and abalone shells on the beach. The ocean was warm and picturesque with turquoise-blue water.

Gerard and Holly witnessed a magnificent, brilliant sunset emerging near the horizon. Bright crimson colors of red, orange, yellow and pink emerged in the early, evening sky. Gerard and Holly were intrigued with the bright colors. Gerard embraced Holly gently and kissed her passionately. They were glad to be together and they were having a magnificent time. Gerard and Holly continued onto the Big Island of Hawaii to witness active volcanoes. Active, orange-red lava splattered out of the volcanoes.

Gerard and Holly observed Hawaiian fishermen throwing handmade fishing nets into the ocean. These Hawaiian fishermen gathered up fish in their nets. Gerard and Holly walked on the wet, warm sand close to the ocean. They felt warm, ocean waves splash over their feet and legs. They held hands as they walked down the beach. They heard waves crashing to the shore.

Kona is a charming city on the Big Island of Hawaii. Holly and Gerard learned to weave baskets with palm leaves at the Kona Hotel where they stayed. They attended another luau and enjoyed succulent, roast pork, fresh cut, tropical fruit such as bananas, pineapples, mangos and breadfruit. They learned more Hawaiian dances. Gerard and Holly continued to experience magnificent times.

Gerard and Holly continued on to Maui where they observed many surfers surfing on large waves. Some waves were 20 to 40 feet high. Gerard rented a surfboard and surfing suit. He went surfing in the ocean. Holly remained on the beach and she watched Gerard surf. Gerard held on to the large surfboard. He stood up on it and surfed on many waves. He was a good surfer. Holly hoped he wouldn't have an accident, especially since it was their honeymoon. Gerard almost fell several times. He managed to stay on his surfboard. He finally came to shore to be with Holly.

The newlyweds continued to enjoy their honeymoon in the Hawaiian Islands for another week. They traveled to other Hawaiian Islands. When they returned to the mainland they brought photographs to show their family and friends.

—— FIVE ——

HEAVENLY REALMS

Blissful, heavenly realms exist in many dimensions in the Cosmic Plan. The higher Astral Universe is an invisible, inner universe which is more refined and maintains a higher vibration and frequency. This heavenly realm is a perfect duplicate of the Cosmic design. God's perfection exists in perfect creations. Invisible planets exist in the higher astral plane. Flames of violet, blue, pink, gold, green, white and indigo are on the higher astral plane. All creations move and vibrate in perfect unity, harmony and centralization. The law of love exists everywhere. Pure love holds God's love in all creations. The more pure love flowing in living creations, the more perfect these creations are in the Cosmic plan.

Heavenly beings may not look human. They may be different Cosmic shapes with spiritual colors. Spiritual beings are far more advanced. They live by Cosmic laws to promote harmony, unity, purity and oneness.

There are many universes in the Cosmic Plan. Each universe may affect other universes. Some universes may merge with other universes. Some universes may be parallel to one another. More advanced universes protect less evolved universes. New universes with developing solar systems are being created so they gradually evolve and become perfect in time.

Heavenly realms maintain an immaculate matrix of the Divine Creator's creations. We have the opportunity to evolve so we can go to heavenly realms in the Great Central Sun which is beyond our physical Sun.

Heaven has been described as pillars of blazing flames with a golden pathway. An etheric globe pulsates near a central altar. The throne of God blazes in the Great Central Sun. Higher, celestial beings move around attached to silver cords. They are pure, peaceful and exist in harmony. There are schools of learning where celestial beings learn how and why the Cosmic Plan in celestial space exists.

— SIX —

OUR WORLD IS CHANGING

Planet Earth came from the Sun. It is believed that our solar system was created by a "Big Bang." The planets all came from the Sun as they burst from its fire balls.

The Earth began as a fire ball. Gradually the Earth hardened over millions of years. As the Earth cooled it was covered with water. Eventually, large land masses developed all over the planet. In time land masses broke apart forming continents. Each continent forms a specific shape and size. Each continent is in a certain location. The continents continue to move gradually inch by inch.

The climate has changed on Earth over billions of years. The Earth was very hot and a tropical climate existed in ancient times. Large, tropical plants grew on Earth, especially 65 million years ago when the dinosaurs roamed the Earth. Then a large asteroid fell to Earth and moved the North and South Pole out of balance. Dust storms raged across the Earth. Plants and animals were destroyed because of the lack of oxygen and water. Earthquakes cracked the Earth. The Earth continued to change. The landscape kept moving and changing.

New plants, animals and then human beings have evolved on our Earth over many millenniums. As life evolved and changed the Earth was effected by these many changes. The North and South poles may move again in the future. This will change the climate. There may be floods, earthquakes and the continents will continue to move and change. New life will emerge on the Earth's surface as well as in the oceans. The climate may become colder and then in time it will warm up again. The Earth will continue to change.

— SEVEN —

SKY MASER'S VICTORY

Sky Maser was an airplane pilot. He was trained by other pilots in a special pilot training program. Within six months he received a pilot's license. He began flying small planes first. He flew passengers from Los Angeles to San Francisco, California. He also flew from Los Angeles to Santa Maria and San Francisco to San Luis Obispo, California. He became an efficient pilot because he was alert, reliable and prompt at landing on time at airports.

Sky Maser was named after his famous uncle, known as Sky Maser. Sky was outgoing, strong and handsome. He towered over other people because he was 6 feet nine inches in height. He enjoyed hobbies such as hiking, swimming, surfing, boating and he played tennis.

Sky was popular because he had a dynamic personality. He expressed himself very well. He liked to read during his spare time. He read adventure stories, biographies, cartoons, science fiction and documentaries about travels. Sky read a variety of worthwhile books, magazines and newspapers. He kept up with current issues and events. He was well rounded.

Sky Maser met many people because he traveled a lot as an airline pilot. Generally, there were thirty passengers in a small airplane flight. He generally was a pilot for three flights a day on a 10 hour day. He had become an accomplished pilot. He continued to perform as an airline pilot for ten years. He had never been in an airplane accident or fallen to the Earth in an airplane crash.

One day after many years of successful airplane piloting, Sky was transferred to a larger plane which meant he would travel much longer flights. He was scheduled to fly from San Francisco to Greenland and back. The changing climate was challenging because the sky became very cold from Alaska to the upper north region of the hemisphere. It snowed a lot and the air was filled with cold ice.

When it was extremely cold sky had to be even more alert because the blades of the airplane propellers could freeze up easily in the extremely cold atmosphere. He observed the propeller carefully. If it was extremely cold he flew the plane above snow and excess ice. He was cautious and aware when wind currents affected the large airplane.

However, even if Sky and his co-pilot were very cautious and alert the weather was unpredictable. They had to be on the lookout for sudden danger. During their flight to Greenland they flew over Alaska. It began to snow heavily. Sky decided to raise the airplane above the snow clouds. When the airplane was above the snow clouds he continued onto Greenland. He hoped to make a safe landing in Greenland in several hours.

It seemed that the airplane was out of danger. The night sky was dark. The airplane continued to operate as Sky and his co-pilot flew it in a northerly direction. Suddenly, a fierce wind began and the plane began to tilt because of the strong wind. The wind currents swished against the airplane. The 200 passengers and pilots as well as airline hostesses felt the strong wind currents. The passengers were told to fasten their seatbelts.

The strong wind currents continued. The passengers began to become concerned about their safety. Sky and his co-pilot John noticed that the right propeller was jammed and had stopped moving. One engine suddenly burned out. Sky and John became concerned and worried. The airplane was losing its regular power. The airplane was difficult to control. It began gliding downward into the heavy clouds below.

Sky realized that the airplane was losing power and he would have to pilot it carefully to the ground. He directed the plane downward as carefully as he could. It was difficult to control the plane. The airplane continued downward into thick, snowy clouds. The snow dropped onto the exterior of the airplane. More ice formed near the propellers.

The passengers were instructed by Sky, who spoke into a loudspeaker, to put on lifejackets and remain in their seats with their seatbelts on. Sky told them to prepare for a bumpy landing. The passengers were told not to panic.

Sky and John weren't able to see out of the pilots' windows because of the thick snow and ice. Sky checked the direction monitors and he pressed buttons to eject the landing tires. He prepared the airplane the best way he knew how for landing.

The airplane came closer and closer to the surface of the Earth. Sky tried to defrost the pilots' windows in order to see the Earth's surface. He tried to see through the clouds as the airplane approached the ground. The airplane fell down into the ocean between Canada and Greenland. As it landed in the ocean, Sky used the emergency pilot control to land the large airplane in the cold water.

Sky glided the airplane carefully into the ocean. The airplane hit the water hard. The passengers held onto their seats. The airline hostesses told the passengers to prepare to leave the airplane to step into life rafts which were blown up and put into the ocean close to the exit, emergency doors. The passengers walked out of the exit doors in groups and stepped into the life rafts from different exit doors.

Sky and John made sure all the passengers and crew were inside the life rafts. Sky and John were the last to step into the life rafts. The airplane began sinking into the ocean. The passengers had their lifejackets on plus warm coats they were instructed to put on.

Sky spoke to the passengers in all the life rafts with a hand-held loudspeaker so they could hear him. Sky spoke with command. "Remain calm everyone." He looked at a hand compass. He continued, "We are approximately three hundred miles from Greenland. I will call for help at the Greenland Airport. I will request helicopters to pick us up. So, don't worry. Remain in your seating positions and cuddle up to keep as warm as you can.

The passengers were cold from the freezing, cold air. It had stopped snowing for awhile. The ocean was filled with icebergs floating around. The ocean was covered with a lot of ice. The life rafts drifted in the cold ocean. The passengers and the crew tried to keep as warm as possible.

Sky and John were in different life rafts. Sky called the Greenland Airport with his emergency cell phone. At first his cell phone didn't work properly. He tried several times to contact the Greenland Airport. Finally, someone answered Sky's cell phone call. The Greenland Airport officer said, "Hello. Can I help you?" Sky replied, "My flight 642 to Greenland has been stopped because the airplane has fallen into the ocean. I have 200 passengers plus my crew sitting in life rafts in the ocean around three hundred miles south of Greenland.

Please send emergency helicopters to pick up the passengers and crew."

The Greenland Airport officer said, "I will have some helicopters sent to pick up the passengers and crew. Is everyone alright?" Sky replied, "No one has been hurt." The airport attendant answered, "Good. We will get to your rafts as soon as we can. Hold tight!" Sky responded, "Thank you. It is very cold and it might snow again soon. So, hurry!"

Once Sky was done speaking to the airport attendant he announced to the passenger and crew that emergency helicopters would be sent to pick everyone up. It was at least two hours before rescue aircraft flew over the life rafts. Ropes with gliding rescue seats were lowered to the life rafts. One passenger at a time was put into a rescue seat and pulled up to each rescue helicopter. When all the passengers were safely in the rescue helicopter, Sky, John and the crew were taken up into the rescue helicopters.

The life rafts remained in the ocean. The rescue pilots flew Flight 642 passengers and all crew members to Greenland. No one was hurt. Sky was thanked by many passengers for saving their lives. This was a victory for Sky because all the passengers were safe in Greenland. No one was injured and no one was killed. Sky was relieved and glad to be safe and in Greenland.

——— EIGHT ———

HIGHER CONSCIOUSNESS

Higher consciousness is important to develop because if we listen to our Real Self, the still small voice of our higher self, we can learn how to understand and accept our Christ Self. Our higher consciousness is our perfect, higher mind which realizes divine truths and wisdom.

Higher consciousness is God's higher intelligence consciously promoting deeper thoughts with much deeper awareness of God's creations and God reality. Higher consciousness sees and knows what is happening. The higher mind identifies with God consciousness.

Higher consciousness is universal awareness. God's consciousness is One Higher Mind in action to affect everything and everyone. God's all knowing intelligence consciously permeates all creation. Higher consciousness is what changes negative situations so that positive results take place. Higher knowledge is exposed which makes a big difference in comprehending life.

Higher consciousness is eternal and will always exist. Higher consciousness is action creating better conditions. God's universal awareness emanates everywhere.

Higher consciousness can be expressed in the human kingdom because human beings learn to think many thoughts once they have learned to speak specific languages. Human beings can learn to identify with their Real Selves to raise their consciousness.

— NINE —

HIGH CHAIR EXPERIENCE

High chairs are used for toddlers to sit in. This chair was designed for toddlers to sit in. This chair was designed so toddlers are safely seated with an attached, sliding small table placed in the high chair. This chair is built to reach the regular dining room table. A toddler is locked in so the toddler will not fall out of the high chair. High chairs are available at restaurants and cafes and other public places such as church, dining halls.

Mark Holman was a two year old toddler. He was learning gradually how to say a few words such as "Ma Ma", "No" and "Dad Da", etc. During feeding times Mark was placed in a high chair. Often he was handed a baby bottle with warm milk. He began sucking the milk. His mother had fastened the high chair table to the high chair so she could place food on this high chair table.

Mark didn't like to sit in a high chair. He preferred to crawl around and walk around to grab food on the dining room table where his parents, brother and sisters were eating their food. Mark would grab food out of his brothers and sisters plates to eat. His brothers and sisters told him to stop grabbing their food to eat. Mark continued to grab food and run away to eat it.

Mark's father knew Mark needed to overcome this bad habit of taking food away from his brothers and sisters. Mark's father rushed after Mark and picked him up. He put the two year old toddler in his high chair and locked him in it. Mark was unable to get out of the high chair. He was very frustrated because he felt trapped in this chair.

Mark began to scream loudly. He took a plastic cup and banged it up and down very loudly on his table tray to express his frustration and anger. Mark had a tantrum while he was locked into the high chair. He kicked his legs up and down and finally he threw the plastic cup he was banging across the dining room swiftly toward his father.

Mark's father walked over to Mark and he took him out of his high chair. He carried Mark out of the dining room to Mark's bed room. He placed Mark over his lap and spanked him firmly. Mark began to cry. Mark's father spanked him on his rear six times to punish Mark for his behavior. Mark continued to cry. He knew his father had punished him for his naughty behavior.

Mark's father put Mark in his crib. He spoke to Mark firmly. "You will have to stay here in your room because you have been naughty!" Mark was still crying because he had been spanked and put to bed. Mark's father walked out of Mark's bedroom. Mark was left alone in his room. He kept crying for another ten minutes. No one came to calm him down. He finally stopped crying. He had laid down in his crib and sucked his thumb. He finally fell asleep because he was exhausted from crying. He wasn't given any attention in his room because he was isolated from his parents, brothers and sisters.

The next morning Mark woke up in his crib. He played with a hanging, dangling mobile above his crib. His other toys were in large boxes near side walls. Mark decided to crawl out of his crib. He climbed over the crib siding and jumped to the floor. He went over to his toy box and took different toys out to play with.

Mark's mother came into his room at about 7:30 a.m. to check on him. She saw him playing with his toys. She changed his diaper and dressed him. She took him into the kitchen near the dining room. She put him in his high chair. She began feeding Mark applesauce, sliced bananas, and scrambled eggs. She encouraged him to drink a cup of milk. Mark didn't fuss or start a tantrum. He ate all of his breakfast. He was hungry because he hadn't eaten much dinner the night before.

After breakfast Mark's mother took him out of the high chair and let him play in a side, lounge room. He climbed on a rocking horse and pretended to ride a real horse. Mark's mother took him outside in the backyard to play and run around. Mark had learned to walk. He was able to play in the sand piles. He enjoyed playing with wet sand. He made sand balls, mud cakes and mud pies. His mother watched Mark play by himself.

When it was time to go in Mark followed his mother into the house. He didn't have anymore tantrums. Mark knew he would probably be spanked again if he caused another big, tantrum outburst.

——— TEN ———

APPEARANCES

Life may not appear to be the way it seems. Appearances may be deceiving. A person may hallucinate when he or she is walking across a hot, arid desert. He or she may see images in the distance which do not exist. People may appear to be behaving in a charming manner. Yet, behind closed doors they may behave in an unpleasant and uninteresting manner. Some couples may appear to be very happy together when they are in public places being observed by other people. In private, they may fight and be incompatible.

Harrison Gibbs was an explorer, photographer and artist. He traveled to unusual places around the world. He brought camping equipment and several cameras. He often took photographs of different, scenic locations. His photographs were sent to travel magazines with articles about different travel experiences. The photographs were very impressive.

People who read the travel magazines were very impressed with the scenic photographs especially. Yet, when Harrison Gibbs photographed specific, scenic views he avoided photographing slums, messy cluttered places and other, uninteresting places which were close to the scenic regions. Readers, who saw the magnificent photographs of the scenic views, were not made aware of the nearby slums and uninteresting places. It appeared that the scenic views were all that existed.

Harrison Gibbs traveled to Jamaica in the Caribbean Islands. This tropical island had many, scenic views of tropical beaches, coves and tropical jungles. It appeared to be a very prosperous, tropical island because only photographs were taken of the scenic locations. When tourists go to Jamaica they find out that many Jamaicans are living in poverty. They live in impoverished looking huts and old, rusty roofed houses. They live in squalor and unscenic locations in Jamaica. Tourists find out that many Jamaicans are unemployed or receive very little money for part time jobs.

Harrison Gibbs traveled to Morocco in Africa. He filmed interesting scenes of Moroccans in outdoor markets selling their artifacts, fruits, vegetables and other goods. The marketplace looked colorful and interesting. However, outside of Moroccan towns and oases the landscape is very arid and unscenic. Dust storms blow across the desert. It is very hot and dry in Morocco. So, Morocco may not be so picturesque in person even if photographs indicate it is beautiful and a pleasant place to live.

Harrison Gibbs continued traveling to different locations. He went to Australia. He photographed scenes in Sydney and the Gold Coast. He traveled to Brisbane and Melbourne. He took many photographs of scenery that was picturesque such as clusters of trees, waterfalls, parks, pristine beaches, sunsets over the ocean and surfers surfing in the ocean.

However, when Harrison Gibbs traveled to the Outback in Australia he observed dry, hot, arid deserts. There were no waterfalls and that landscape was not nearly as scenic. Yet, his scenic photographs made Australia appear to be very scenic. Tourists, who traveled through the Outback, have also observed hot, dry, arid landscapes which was not as scenic.

What may appear to look very scenic and interesting may not look quite the same in person as in photographs in magazines, newspapers and books. Photographers usually photograph the most scenic views of different locations to impress their readers.

—— ELEVEN ——

MARIE MONTESSORI'S EDUCATIONAL METHODS

Marie Montessori was raised in Italy by wealthy parents who encouraged her to become a doctor. She was the first woman physician in Italy in the early 20th Century. Marie Montessori observed poverty-stricken children who lived in slum areas in Rome, Italy.

Marie Montessori was concerned about children being deprived of a good education. Marie decided to collect tangible materials which she put into shelves in trays. Miniature objects were labeled with name tags. Marie Montessori selected a basement in a large house to experiment with progressive, Montessori methods.

Marie Montessori made shelves along each wall and she placed a variety of tangible, educational material in every shelf. She made tables for children to sit at. She had a section for children to paint at an easel. She also put a chalkboard in the large, basement room.

Then, Marie Montessori began gathering children from slum areas in Rome. She gathered at least fifty children to attend her new, progressive school. The children were allowed to select tangible, educational materials in given trays to work with.

The shelves were classified by specific topics. There was a section for cooking and dining skills, personal graces, social graces, geography materials, mathematical materials and reading materials. Children were allowed to select specific tangible materials to take to the tables. They were shown by Marie Montessori and her assistants how to use these hands on, tangible materials.

Marie Montessori taught the children in her school to learn by doing. Learning to use tangible materials is the best way to learn about specific subjects. The children were much more motivated to learn. They were allowed to pick and choose what they were interested in. They made decisions when they chose specific materials to learn about.

Children sat at different tables learning to use different, Montessori, tangible materials. They learned much faster on a one to one basis. They also sat in groups while Marie Montessori demonstrated how to use different, tangible, educational materials.

Marie Montessori developed concepts which she wrote about. She developed concepts such as the receptive mind, the absorbent mind, the inductive and deductive mind and collective mind. She wrote about each of these concepts. The Marie Montessori methods of learning has been published. Marie Montessori has written a number of books about her progressive methods of education.

The Marie Montessori methods of learning eventually spread to other countries such as Holland, India, Ceylon and America. It was discovered that the children in Marie Montessori's school were learning much earlier and faster how to read, write and learn mathematics and geography much better and sooner.

The Montessori methods of learning has spread all over the world. Adults are trained at Montessori Institutes the Montessori methods of learning. They develop lesson plans for all the Montessori methods. Social graces are presented. Children learn to say thank you, please, hello and goodbye, etc. They learn to take off their sweaters and coats to hang up. They learn to fold napkins, set the table, wash and dry dishes, sweep floors and put tangible materials away in the shelves.

Children from the age of three on learn social graces as well as how to use the many hands-on-materials. They may select whatever they are interested in learning about. There are blocks, puzzles, pyramids, clay to mold, paint for finger painting, etc., to enjoy playing with. Blocks can be used to build block bridges, houses, cars, pyramids and many more creative projects. Children are allowed to use their imagination to be creative and spontaneous.

Children, who go to Montessori Schools, increase their intelligence at an earlier age. They learn a variety of skills using hands-on materials. They become more self sufficient and adaptable in creative, stimulating Montessori classrooms. They learn to read, write, think and understand academic subjects with more comprehension. They become more productive as well as independent while they are learning a variety of skills and academic subjects.

—— TWELVE ——

WHY PEOPLE SHAVE

People shave because they don't want hair to grow on their faces. Men generally shave with an electric shaver or use razor blades to shave their facial hair off.

Some men have mustaches and beards. They taper their mustaches and trim their beards to look well groomed. Some men shave under their arms. Some men even shave their legs so their legs will look smoother.

Women usually shave under their arms. They also shave their legs with electric shavers, or with razor blades. Some women use hair cream which causes hair on their legs to come off. They wash under their arms and they wash their legs. They usually apply hand cream to keep their skin from drying out.

People think they look much better and more groomed when they remove unwanted hair from their faces, under their arms and on their legs. Shaving equipment should be kept clean. Do not share the same razor blades with someone else. Keep shaving equipment in a safe, dry place.

Some men and even some women shave the hair off their heads. They apply hand cream on their shaved heads to keep their scalps smooth and shiny. Some people shave only part of their hair off to create a Mohawk look. They may have a long braid in the back while they are bald on the rest of their heads.

People will continue to shave in order to remove unwanted hair. They want to look a certain way in order to attract other people. Having too much hair or not enough hair is unattractive. People want to maintain a certain appearance to be appreciated and attractive to others. Hair styles are important. Hair is shaved off a person's neck. Electric shavers and scissors are used to taper sideburns and hair on the back of the head. People want to look their best.

────── THIRTEEN ──────

EXPERIENCES DURING SCHOOL DAYS

We have many memories of our school days. We usually remember who our teachers were from primary school, elementary school and high school. Some of the teachers impressed us much more than other teachers. Some teachers had a sense of humor while other teachers scolded us and were very strict. We remember classmates and friends we made in school. We went to school parties, plays, variety shows and PTA programs. We remember going through each grade. We learned specific skills in each grade level.

Sarah Long remembered her school days. She attended Avila Beach Elementary School and Arroyo Grande High School. She recalled the names of her elementary school teachers and even many of her high school teachers.

Sarah was popular in elementary and high school. She was able to make friends readily. She socialized with her friends during lunch breaks and recesses. She attended after school activities and events. Sarah joined in physical education games such as kickball, baseball, basketball, volleyball and tennis. Sarah was a good game player as well as a good sport when she lost a game. She was athletically coordinated and physically fit. She even joined Cheerleaders when she attended high school. She wore a cheerleading outfit. She used pom poms to shake in the air.

Sarah Long was talented as a vocal soloist and pianist. She also learned to play the clarinet and oboe. She participated in the high school band. The Arroyo Grande High School band participated in the Harvest Festival Parade, Fourth of July Parade, Christmas Parade and Santa Maria Rodeo Parade. Sarah wore a colorful, band outfit and band hat. She played her clarinet as she marched in the high school band. Photographs and videos were taken of the Arroyo Grande High School Band marching and playing in different parades. Photographs were shown in the local newspapers. Original photographs were displayed on bulletin boards at the high school and downtown on outdoor and indoor bulletin boards. Sarah could be seen in the photographs playing in the marching band.

Sarah attended junior high school and high school dances. She dressed up in her favorite dress and she styled her hair in a more glamorous manner before she attended each dance. Sarah was asked to dance frequently by different high school boys. The high school boys dressed up in suits, ties and dress shoes.

Sarah was a good dancer. She was capable of dancing a variety of dance steps. She looked good on the dance floor with each guy she danced with. She enjoyed dancing jitterbug, waltzes and Spanish style dancing. The school dances began at 7 p.m. and ended at 11 p.m. Sarah was given a ride home by her dates to dances. She maintained her self control when any guy approached her for sex. She wanted to preserve her reputation as a moral person. She didn't want to get pregnant out of wedlock. Sarah planned to go to college after she graduated from high school. She planned to become a high school Social Studies and Language Arts teacher.

Sarah went to school and back home on the school bus. She often sat with different high school friends on the buses. She socialized on the bus. She talked about her school teachers, classes and about what she was learning about in high school. She liked to read a lot. So, she often spoke about different novels and nonfiction books she was reading. She expressed her opinions and details about books she had finished reading.

Sarah was allowed to use school computers in different classrooms at the high school. She learned a lot when she turned on Google. She could look up a variety of subjects and topics. She received important information to write reports and theses as well as essays. She was able to receive an A on her research papers because she gathered current, pertinent information from Google on the internet.

Sarah was a well rounded person. She was successful in her academic subjects as well as in music and sports. She had a bright future ahead of her. In her senior year of high school she applied at different, accredited colleges. She was required to take entrance exams. She waited to hear the results of these exams.

Several months went by and Sarah finally received the results of each entrance exam. She had passed all the entrance exams. She received entrance applications from six accredited universities. She decided to attend Stanford University in Palo Alto, California. Sarah treasured her memories of elementary and high school. However, she looked forward to attending college soon.

—— FOURTEEN ——

UNUSUAL EXPERIENCES

It takes courage and determination to surpass difficult times. A person must learn to face many crises and problems during different stages of one's life. Meaningful values and purposes can help a person surpass difficult times.

Terry Atkins was a physically fit person. He was able to drive vehicles on busy freeways and dangerous, mountain roads. Terry had been driving for twenty years. He had never been in an accident all those years. He had taken many people from one place to another year after year. Terry had saved money for twenty years. He wanted to live in an attractive, spacious house with a spectacular view of the ocean.

Terry Atkins anticipated a pleasant, safe future in which he could be prosperous and physically fit. Little did he know he would be encountering serious, future difficulties. He was driving a passenger van over a mountain pass one day when the road became very narrow on a steep incline. There were heavy rocks that suddenly fell down to the narrow, dangerous road. Some of the heavy rocks fell on to the top of the passenger van. Some of the tumbling rocks blocked the narrow road.

The passenger van skidded on this steep incline which had no guard rails or fence. Terry tried to control the van. The wheels kept skidding. The van was stuck between large rocks. Terry had two passengers sitting in passenger seats behind his driver's seat. The van was stuck on the isolated, mountain road. Terry tried to move the van passed the rock-filled road. It was impossible for him to drive it any further.

The two passengers, Billy Wrango, and Sally Preston became upset and began to panic. Terry tried to calm them down. Terry got out of the van to look around. He hoped to find a way to drive the van away from the rubble. Terry decided to carry the rocks on the road away from the van. He asked his two passengers to help him lift rocks and to help carry them to the side of the narrow road so there would be enough room to drive the van back down the narrow road. The big rocks were difficult to move. So Terry, Billy and Sally lifted one rock at a time together.

It took several hours to remove the heavy rocks to the side of the narrow road. By the time the rocks were removed it had gotten dark. It was a moonless night. Terry decided not to drive on this dangerous road high in the mountains at night. He knew it was very dangerous to drive on this narrow incline in the dark.

Terry told his two passengers that they would have to sleep in the van that night. They didn't have bedrolls. There were two blankets in the back of the van. Terry took the blankets out of the back of the van. He handed a blanket to Sally and a blanket to Billy. Terry would not have a blanket to keep him warmer during the cold night.

Billy Wrango and Sally Preston only had some snacks such as nuts and some fruit to eat and canned foods. Terry had packed a lunch box with a bologna sandwich with lettuce, sliced tomatoes and sliced pickles on rye bread. Mustard was spread on the rye bread. There was an apple and several oatmeal cookies. Terry had containers of coffee to drink. Sally, Billy and Terry were hungry because they had spent hours lifting heavy rocks to move to the side of the road.

Terry suggested that it was time to eat whatever food they all brought with them. So, Sally, Billy and Terry took their available food out and began eating. They sat in the van while they ate. The food they ate would have to sustain them until they were back to civilization down below the mountain. They began eating their food. They sipped their beverages.

After eating what food the three travelers had brought with them they were going to have to sleep in the van that night. It had gotten very chilly. Sally put on her jacket and wrapped her blanket around her to try to keep warmer. Billy was wearing a jacket. He also wrapped up in the blanket he was given.

The back seats were adjustable. Terry adjusted the seats so they could be lowered into flat surfaces and used beds. Billy and Sally decided to lay down on the adjusted seats with their blankets around them. Terry opened several windows partially so fresh air could come inside the van.

Terry adjusted his front seat into a bed shape. He put on a long, warm coat to cover over his body. The temperature continued to drop during the night. The temperature dropped to 15 degrees F. Terry tried to rest. However, he was very uncomfortable because he was shivering because he felt very cold.

Around 12:20 a.m. Terry heard some strange sounds nearby. The van doors were closed. Only the windows were partially open. Terry sat up and looked outside the van windows. He saw a flashing, glowing object coming down from the sky. Terry continued to watch the glowing object which appeared to be a UFO.

Terry saw the object fall to the mountainside several miles in the distance. The object was still glowing when it landed on the mountainside. Terry was very curious about this glowing object. He decided to get out of the van and walk into the direction of the glowing, unknown object.

It was very cold outside. Yet, Terry continued to walk up the narrow mountain road. His fingers and toes began to freeze. Yet, he continued to walk further up the mountain road. He came closer and closer to the glowing object. Finally, he came very close to the UFO. Terry saw a pulsating orange and yellow light emanating from a cylinder-shaped object which appeared to be made out of refined metal. There were hieroglyphics carved on this cylinder object.

Terry walked up to this fallen object. He attempted to touch the surface of the object. When he attempted to touch it his fingers were burnt. He pulled his hand away quickly from the strange glowing object. It was completely covered with a special metallic surface. Terry didn't have a camera. He wished he could take photographs of this object to show other people. The object kept glowing. It was approximately 15 feet long by 10 feet wide.

Suddenly, the cylinder opened on one end. Terry stood there wondering what would happen. Two short human-like beings walked out of the cylinder. They saw Terry standing near the cylinder object. The two alien beings were wearing silver space suits with helmets. Their faces could be seen through a clear, plastic covering.

Terry stared at the two little human-like beings. He was 6 foot 2 inches tall. They were around 3 feet, four inches tall. They were not carrying weapons. Terry felt somewhat afraid of them because he realized they were from another planet. He didn't run away. He stood there wondering what these two outer space beings would do now that they saw him.

The two celestial beings stood there looking at Terry. They didn't appear to be afraid. The first one spoke in a high pitched voice. The first celestial being said, "Greetings. We come from far away. Who are you?" Terry was very surprised this outer space being could speak English. He replied, "Where do you come from?" The celestial being answered, "We have traveled millions of miles across space. We are from Travia in celestial space."

Terry continued to stand there. These outer space beings didn't seem to be harmful or dangerous. Terry spoke, "I am from this planet Earth. I don't know where Travia is." The second celestial being spoke in a high pitched voice. "Travia is in the constellation Pleiades. We have traveled quite a long distance." Terry responded, "Welcome to Earth. I didn't expect to meet anyone from outer space tonight. My van is down the road from here. I couldn't drive during the night on this narrow road." The first celestial being spoke. "We have been on your planet before. We were running out of energy in our space mobile. So, we landed here. We will have to regenerate our energy before we go back out into space."

Terry realized that these little men seemed very human as well as friendly. He didn't expect to have such an unusual experience encountering celestial beings from so far away. The first celestial being said, "We must be going now, We have more places to travel to in space. Goodbye." The two little celestial beings walked back into their spaceship.

The spaceship began pulsating very brightly for a few minutes. Terry stepped away from this space vehicle. It suddenly lifted up from the mountain road and moved swiftly up into the sky and quickly traveled away. It disappeared within one minute.

Terry stood there amazed at what he saw and experienced. He finally walked back to the van. He stepped into the van. He laid down to rest. He thought about the two celestial beings and their space craft.

The next morning Terry drove the van back down the mountain road with the two passengers. He told them what he had experienced during the night. They didn't believe what he had told them about the celestial beings and their space craft. Terry had no photographs to prove what he had experienced that night.

── FIFTEEN ──

PRESIDENTIAL SECRETS

Each American President has kept secrets while he was in office. They wanted to keep certain political and personal problems private in order to avoid scandals and unkind gossip which could affect their image and reputation. Many things are exposed about each American president especially years after they have completed their terms as President of the United States of America.

George Washington, the first American President, did not reveal his personal life to his followers and soldiers. He was a private person. He married Martha, who was a wealthy widow. They never had any children. They lived at Mount Vernon.

Thomas Jefferson, the third American President, traveled to England and France as an ambassador of America before he became an American President. He had an intimate relationship with one of his female, black slaves. In the early days intermarriage was unheard of and unaccepted in America. Jefferson's black mistress gave birth to at least six offspring, who grew up at Jefferson Estate. This was kept secret for many years.

Woodrow Wilson was an American President in 1915. He became very ill during his term in office. His wife tried to cover-up his illness. She often took over and made decisions in which her husband was supposed to make. Woodrow Wilson formed the League of Nations. He wanted to unite world countries. Unfortunately, the League of Nations failed to carry out its mission.

Abraham Lincoln, our sixteenth American President, ran in two American elections before he became an American President. His wife, Mary Todd Lincoln, encouraged Abraham Lincoln to run for the American Presidency. Abraham Lincoln didn't want to become President of America. His wife was very ambitious. She wanted to marry someone who would become President of America.

Many American Presidents joined secret societies such as the Free Masons. George Washington was the first of at least 15 Masons who were elected presidents of the United States of America. The Illuminati masterminded the French Revolution. It also infiltrated Continental Freemasonic lodges and threatened the stability of Europe. Americans feared that the group's radical ideas would soon cross the Atlantic. Fortunately, it never happened.

Some secret societies, in general, have gained a reputation as a pernicious influence. A subjection of them have, at times, played a beneficial role in human history.

George Walker Bush is the third Bonesman to be elected President of the United States after William H. Taft and George H.W. Bush. Two Skull and Bonesmen, George W. Bush and John F. Kerry, ran against each other for President of the U.S.A.

John F. Kennedy investigated inflation in America. He questioned why the American dollar lost at least 50 percent of its value. He found out that at least six, underground, wealthy financial organizations were secretly in power. These six financial groups were controlling the American economy. Because of John F. Kennedy's careful investigation, he was assassinated in November, 1963. His brother, Robert Kennedy, was also assassinated for trying to follow through by attempting to make changes to improve the economy and political image of America during the 1960s.

The American public were not informed the real reasons John F. Kennedy and his brother, Robert Kennedy were assassinated. It took several decades before the real reasons were revealed. Ted Kennedy decided not to run as a candidate for President of America after what happened to his two brothers, John and Robert Kennedy.

It has become known in the last twenty years that American presidents are secretly influenced and controlled by an underground, Illuminati group. Different American presidents have been influenced and controlled by powerful financial groups. The American public, in general, are not aware of these secret, power groups.

American presidents continued to keep many secrets in order to avoid scandals and unkind gossip. These secrets have been kept so the American presidents could avoid criticism and being forced out of office. Presidential secrets will continue to be kept as long as secret power groups exist.

SIXTEEN

WORTHWHILE ENDEAVORS

There are many worthwhile endeavors to pursue. Some people volunteer to work for the Red Cross. Other people enroll in the Peace Corp. Some individuals donate money to worthwhile, service organizations such as CARE Incorporated, UNESCO and different charitable groups.

The Christian Women collect canned goods and packaged, dried foods to give to needy people who need food. Shelters are provided for homeless people. Some churches provide one, daily free meal during noontime to feed unemployed as well as homeless people.

Employers, who create new jobs for unemployed people, are providing these people an opportunity to work to earn a regular living. Unemployed people should have an opportunity to work in order to pay their bills. People need to be able to be employed in order to survive.

Receiving certain academic and specific training to obtain certain jobs is a worthwhile endeavor. When ten percent or more people are unemployed they are put in a position to collect unemployment. They must depend on others in order to help them survive.

Many homeless people struggle because they need safe shelters to dwell in plus enough food to stay alive. Anyone who donates food, clothing and adequate shelter is helping needy people to help them, especially when these needy people are down and out.

When needy people ask for help be kind and generous to them. Encourage them to keep looking for employment. Tell them not to give up. There may be employment available which may help unemployed individuals become employed. So, continue to help the needy people. This may make a real difference in their lives.

— SEVENTEEN —

SHIPS AT SEA

When you walk down to a seaport harbor usually large ships are seen anchored in the ocean. There are passenger ships that take tourists on long cruises. Cargo ships carry exports, imports and a variety of merchandise and goods to far away places.

Ships at sea have many miles to travel across the ocean. Ships must be able to withstand storms at sea. Ships must be able to stay afloat in order to travel long distances across the vast ocean.

Some ships are operated by electricity. Other ships are operated by burning coal. Old fashion ships navigated with large sails. Many ships today have four or five levels or decks. The ship's captain and crew stay in a certain level of the ship. Passengers stay in passenger quarters. Many passenger cabins have window views and usually there are two beds in a cabin.

Passenger ships line up at piers to pick up passengers. A long plank is connected from the ship to the pier. Passengers are able to walk across the plank to shore.

Passengers' luggage is brought to shore either by porters or hoisted down by carrier pulleys.

Ships usually stay in harbors for a period of time so cargo can be taken off and new cargo can be put on. Heavy cargo and large loads of accumulated luggage are lifted up into the ships on long ropes with pulleys. Cruise ships remain in harbors until all the passengers and crew are safely on them. Cruise ships must be re-supplied with enough food to be prepared and served to the passengers and crew. Other supplies are also stored such as medical equipment, blankets, sheets and pillow cases, etc.

Once a ship has been properly supplied and all necessary luggage is put aboard the ship leaves the harbor to travel to its assigned destination across the ocean.

A variety of ships and vessels can be seen in many harbors. People and sailors depend on large ships to sail across the ocean to other harbors in distant places. People look forward to taking long cruises to interesting, scenic places in the world. Ships are seen traveling in the sea throughout many months each year. Many people enjoy long cruises across the sea. Vivid sunrises and sunsets can be seen while you travel by ships in the ocean. It is worth traveling to distant locations by cruise ships. Cargo ships are very necessary to carry important cargo to distant harbors.

—— EIGHTEEN ——

THE SCHOLAR

Ryan Collins was very intelligent from primary grades and throughout elementary and high school. He was an A student in every grade. Ryan was an excellent scholar throughout school.

Ryan decided to attend Yale University after he graduated from high school. He had learned to write research papers, sophisticated essays, informative articles, poetry and novels. Ryan was an excellent writer. He also expressed himself quite well in conversations, discussion groups and when he presented speeches. Ryan participated in debates. He was able to present pros and cons when he participated in different debates.

Yale University is a well known, accredited university in America. Ryan looked forward to attending this well established university. Ryan received a scholarship fund to help him pay for tuition and books while he attended Yale. He also received a trust fund from his parents. Ryan moved into one of the dorms at Yale University.

Ryan shared a dorm room with another freshman when he moved into the dorm. He stayed on the third floor in a dorm room with two single beds, several dressers and a large closet. Ryan shared the closet with his roommate. His roommate's name was Will Stover. Will moved into the dorm room about the same time as Ryan moved in.

Classes began after Labor Day in September at Yale University. Ryan selected a major in Sociology and a minor in Speech. He enrolled in General Education for the first two years of college because these courses were required first. Ryan took 15 units each quarter. He was able to study to prepare for each exam. Ryan also wrote research papers for different courses such as Social Science, Economics, Logic, English, Anthropology, Speech and Biology, etc.

Ryan was a top scholar during his college days at Yale University. He participated in debates and he presented excellent speeches. He wrote articles for the Yale University newspaper and journal. Ryan had a very high I.Q. In fact, Ryan was a genius.

Ryan finally graduated from Yale University with a B.S. in Sociology with a minor in Speech. He continued working on a Masters Degree and then a Ph.D. in Sociology. He worked on a Ph.D. which was about "Behavioral Patterns of Human Beings." Ryan made a careful study of how different age groups behave when experiencing stressful situations. His Ph.D. thesis became a successful, original document. His thesis was filed at Yale University with the Sociology Department. Ryan presented his Ph.D. thesis to the graduate school thesis committee. They were quite impressed with Ryan Collin's presentation of his original thesis.

Ryan presented specific observations about toddlers 1-4, ages 4-11, teenagers 13-19 and young adults, 20-25. He described how these age groups behave when they are experiencing stress and anxiety. Ryan found out that toddlers are programmed by their parents, brothers and sisters to become stressful and anxious because of undue influence. They are taught to be afraid of spiders, snakes and gorillas, etc. If they have not been told to stay away from spiders and snakes many toddlers do not act frightened of them.

Ryan continued to describe the behavior of 4 year olds up to 12 year olds. He stated that four year olds, five year olds, six year olds, seven year olds, etc. tend to imitate their parents, brothers and sisters. They develop the same habits and basic characteristics of their elders, who have a strong influence on them. Children tend to acquire certain attitudes because of their daily environment. They learn how to respond according to the responses of those around them. Customs and beliefs are learned over a period of time. Attitudes are formed over years of influence. Every individual is influenced by the behavior of immediate relatives, friends, teachers and ministers.

Ryan studied the way teenagers behave. He observed how emotional they behave and especially the way they respond to one another. He found out that many teenagers are sexually aroused by the opposite sex, especially from the age of 16 to 19. The hormones in the bodies of teenagers are changing during this physical growth period. Some teenagers, who live secluded lives, may behave differently than teenagers who are influenced by their peers. They respond to the behavior of others.

Ryan Collins finally stated his conclusions about human behavior. He eventually wrote a lengthy book about different, human behavior of specific age groups. Ryan continued to be a scholar. Ryan observed the differences of older and younger generations. Older generations believed in the importance of marriage. So, children born would have the legal names and protection of their fathers. Yet, young adults from the age of 18 to 40 do not think marriage is necessary or important. Younger generations are not concerned about what older generations think about the importance of marriage.

Ryan spoke to many divorced couples. He found out that divorced couples did not want to get married again. They don't want to pay alimony and child support. Many divorced men have had to move out of nice homes while their divorced wives remained in these homes. They become bitter because they end up living in a small apartment instead. Divorced men are forced to pay a lot of money for child support and alimony.

Therefore, they have little money left for their personal needs. So, the idea of getting married again is not a desirable choice. Divorced men are willing to have affairs. They are willing to live with women they desire to be intimate with. They refuse to make a legal commitment.

Ryan found out that children are affected by the divorce of their parents. Children often suffer a lot when their parents break up. They must learn to accept the separation of their parents. Many children experience a lot of stress and anxiety when their parents break up and get divorced. They must learn to cope with the challenges in their homes. This effects their behavior in their homes, at school and in the community.

Ryan continued to study the social behavior of different age groups. He observed that human beings desire to live in communities and ethnic groups. Human beings need to feel a sense of belonging and security. Human beings need shelter, food and protection. Human beings depend on each other to strengthen their economic standing and social needs. Human beings learn to communicate by speaking different languages. They live in families. Human beings desire to reproduce offspring to promote future generations. Ryan concluded that human beings will continue to behave a certain way in each generation. Ryan Collins wrote a bestseller entitled BEHAVIOR IN EACH GENERATION. He was a recognized established scholar.

— NINETEEN —

WHY CERTAIN STORES SUCCEED

Certain stores are very successful in cities, communities, villages and towns. Why do some stores succeed over a long period of time? Stores that are very successful generally have a wide variety of merchandise. These stores usually have reasonable prices so that customers can afford to buy merchandise. These stores become chains and they are attractive and have worthwhile products.

Wal-Mart has been very successful for many years. Wal-Mart has a wide variety of desirable merchandise. The prices are very reasonable so many people come to Wal-Marts to buy a variety of things they want and need. Wal-Marts continue to grow and expand. There are many Wal-Mart stores in America.

Woolworths Department Store was established in the 1930s. Woolworths has a wide variety of merchandise. The prices have been very reasonable. Large cities such as New York City, Chicago, San Francisco and Los Angeles still have Woolworths stores.

J.C. Penny is another successful store. J.C. Pennys has expanded and exists around the U.S.A. Pennys is known for a variety of clothes and household items. Sears and Roebucks is another successful store. Sears and Roebucks is known for kitchen appliances such as stoves, refrigerators, toasters, microwave ovens and kitchen utensils such as electric frying pans, pots and pans, silverware and many items.

Macys is another well known store with quality clothes and many other items. Macys has existed for many years. It probably will continue to be a successful store for many years to come.

Successful stores are well planned. Reasonable prices exist so many people can afford to buy the merchandise. Successful stores continue to find ways to stay open and to expand their business in order to make enough money to stay open for many years.

— TWENTY —

UPHOLDING FREEDOM

Freedom is very necessary and important in order for humanity to be fulfilled. The pursuit of liberty and happiness is experienced when human beings are free to experience what they want in life.

Many people came to America to seek freedom, liberty and justice. Freedom is maintained when individuals fulfill their goals and ambitions. Without freedom individuals do not experience happiness and fulfillment.

Everyone has an opportunity to be free. Freedom must be earned and even fought for. Freedom brings joy and spontaneity to individuals. We need to uphold freedom for our lives. We will be able to complete our best plans and dreams. Each fulfilled goal and dream will bring individuals a worthwhile life.

───── TWENTY-ONE ─────

DICTATORSHIPS THAT FELL

In ancient Rome different emperors became dictators. Some of these dictators were Herotitus, Nero, Julius Caesar, Octavius and Augustus. Each of these dictators dictated what Roman laws and policies were to be accepted. Roman people were expected to obey whatever the dictators wanted them to do.

Herotitus established the Roman Coliseum, where Roman gladiators were expected to fight until death. Even if there was a Roman Senate, the senators had to please the emperors. Some senators were banished and other senators were murdered and deliberately killed because they didn't abide by the emperor's wishes and expectations.

Herotitus built bridges and beautiful, architectural buildings. He promoted art, poetry and cultural events. However, he was hated and despised by certain Romans. He was murdered eventually. Nero became a Roman emperor. He had fanatical notions and he murdered his mother and his wife because he didn't trust them.

He didn't want his offspring to take his place. Nero actually went insane and he ordered his soldiers to burn down Rome. Then he blamed the early Christians for the burning of Rome. He had early Christians executed in the Roman Coliseum to cover up for his decision to have Rome burned. In time, the Roman people found out that Nero ordered Rome to be burned down. Nero eventually killed himself when he knew the Roman people planned to punish and kill him for his evil acts.

Octavius became another dictator after Julius Caesar was assassinated in Rome. Octavius captured Cleopatra, the last Egyptian leader. Octavius was merciless to Christians and anyone who didn't obey his commands. In time, Octavius also fell. He eventually was called Augustus and he ruled longer than any other Roman emperors.

Rome finally fell because many of the emperors, who were dictators, were corrupt. They were self centered and very selfish. Many of the emperors were possessed by evil spirits. They had Roman legions capture many people in other countries. Their captors were chained and forced into slavery and bondage. Thousands of people became slaves of the Roman Empire.

Rome fell within approximately four hundred years after Jesus Christ was crucified. Constantine became the first Christian emperor. He tried to establish justice. He attempted to be a fair ruler. He listened to the Roman senators and accepted suggestions. A new Roman government was established under his rule.

Adolph Hitler was a dictator in Germany, Austria, Holland, Poland, Czechoslovakia and France. He also tried to take over in Russia. Hitler captured six million Jews. He put them in concentration camps. Many Jews were executed in a very cruel manner.

Hitler was possessed by Satanic forces. He hated the Jews. He believed the Aryan race was superior to all other races. German people were thought to be of the Aryan race. Hitler wanted to rule the world. When Americans entered World War II, Hitler and his Nazi regime continued to invade Europe. When Americans fought the Germans they eventually defeated them. Soldiers from England, Russia, India, Africa, Australia and New Zealand fought alongside the Americans in order to win World War II.

Hitler, who was a powerful dictator, was finally defeated. He fell from power in 1945. Many people believe that Hitler committed suicide at the end of the war. Germany finally surrendered. Today, Germans have a democratic government.

Mussolini was an Italian dictator. He dominated Italy for a period of time. He was very demanding. Italians became dissatisfied with Mussolini as a dictator. Mussolini was captured by Italian partisans and he was strung up on a balcony. He was no longer in power. He was no longer dictator of Italy because of his corrupt ways. Unjust, unfair dictators have been removed from power because of their corrupt leadership.

TWENTY-TWO

ATLANTEAN MYSTERIES

Atlantis existed in the Bahamas Islands and to the East in the Atlantic Ocean 12,500 years ago. Atlantis had survived for thousands of years. Then in one day Atlantis fell down in the ocean.

Atlanteans were artistic, poetic and highly philosophical for a long period of time. Atlanteans focused on crystals which blazed with bright light. They designed circular, rock altars. Amethyst stones existed and they were displayed in the Atlantean city.

Atlanteans were mystical people who worshipped nature spirits, gods and goddesses. They discovered the use of electricity and laser beam rays. In fact, laser guns were invented and used to destroy life on Atlantis. If the Atlanteans had maintained peace, harmony and unity the continent of Atlantis may not have fallen in the Atlantic Ocean.

Some Atlanteans migrated from Atlantis to form other European civilizations. Atlanteans had acquired mystical powers which they used for many years. They believed in eternal life.

Socrates, Plato and Edgar Cayce wrote about Atlantis. These writers wrote about the rise and fall of Atlantis.

In 2009 more recently discovered underwater ruins theoretically from Atlantis were explored in the Bahamas Islands. These findings were shown on the History Channel in October, 2009. Diving expeditions by Greg Little, a well-known explorer of ancient ruins, located rectangular buildings, walls and paved roads. The straight lines and even spacing between the structures was evidence these are not natural formations. Geologists estimated the depth of the ocean at this location during the alleged time of Atlantis, and concluded it was then above sea level.

Many other underwater structures attributed to Atlantis have been found on the seafloor near Spain, Morocco, the Azores, the Canary Islands, and across the Atlantis Ocean to the Bahamas and the Caribbean Sea. These discoveries include pyramids, circular buildings, Greek architecture, a blacktop road, a harbor, columns and a city similar to Plato's description. That community was in the zone indicated by Plato for the Atlantean capital city. The ruins and artifacts on the seafloor of the Atlantic Ocean are detailed in my book EXTRATERRESTRIAL CIVILIZATIONS ON EARTH.

TWENTY-THREE

PLAYING TENNIS

Many people learn to play tennis. They are taught how to hold the racket. They must learn how to move on the tennis court. The right action of movement with the tennis racket is important. Coordination, flexibility and timing are necessary in order to play tennis well. Tennis players must learn to hit the tennis ball firmly and accurately over the tennis net during the game.

Tennis matches are played by two players called singles. If four tennis players play this is called doubles. Tennis players wear tennis clothes and tennis shoes to be comfortable. Before tennis matches players generally warm up by hitting tennis balls against a tennis wall to prepare for the tennis game.

Two tennis players who play singles must keep tennis balls within the second inner lines on each side of the court. If the tennis ball hits the net and doesn't go over, the player loses a point. A server is given two chances to serve a tennis ball into the correct court.

Points are added up using love, fifteen, thirty, forty, tie and if another point is made beyond forty the tennis player who earns more than forty, wins the tennis match. If three games are won in sequence the player wins the match.

Tennis players should have enough tennis balls and several good tennis rackets. Tennis is always played on tennis courts which have painted lines to designate specific, boundary lines required to stay in during any tennis match. A good tennis player keeps in good, physical shape. It is important to be a good sport and maintain effective team work with other tennis players. Famous, tennis players have won many tennis matches. They have developed a good reputation as excellent, tennis players.

TWENTY-FOUR

SEEKING TRUTH

Seeking truth is significant because each soul has the opportunity to seek inner wisdom and knowledge. To learn about the cosmic realities of the Divine Creator is part of God's plan. Each soul has the opportunity to evolve and awaken to higher consciousness. Higher consciousness is a stream of continuous thoughts which expand the mind and awaken the soul.

We can learn about universal, Cosmic laws of love, harmony, unity, reincarnation, karma (cause and effect), polarities, magnetism, light, motion, gravitation, attraction and repulsion. Intervals of space and time exist. Many dimensions also exist and there are parallel planes. Most planes are invisible to the physical eyes. The physical plane is only visible to the physical eyes. The physical plane is only one density. Yet, there are many dimensions that affect other dimensions.

How can the soul seek inner truth? Each soul needs to listen to the inner voice of his or her God presence.

One must quiet the outer mind in order to listen to God consciousness. Higher consciousness is pure and perfect. The Divine Creator maintains perfect, higher consciousness. All truth is within the Cosmic stream of higher, supreme consciousness. We can seek eternal, universal truths in our daily lives to awaken to God's eternal creations.

——— TWENTY-FIVE ———

EXISTENTIALISM

Existentialism began in the late 1950s. Sarte developed this philosophy. Existentialism is a philosophical and literary movement, both religious and atheistic, stemming from Kierkegaard and represented by Sarte and Heidegger. It is based on the doctrine that existence takes precedence over essence and holds that man is totally free and responsible for his acts, and that this responsibility is the source of the dread and anguish that encompasses him. Existentialism expresses actuality as opposed to conceptual possibility, stated in WEBSTER'S NEW WORLD DICTIONARY.

Kierkegaard did not believe that God is the Divine Creator. He believed we exist because we exist. He was not aware of God's divine plan. However, he believed we are accountable for all our actions and behavior. We need to learn what is right to do. Wrongdoing will cause suffering and unhappiness.

We learn how to survive and to exist in a world of chaos and confusion. We observe through our physical senses of sight, sound, touch, taste and smell. Our physical senses alert us to what is happening around us.

Sarte and Heidegger followed Kierkegaard's existential philosophy. They were not aware of metaphysical truths. So, they were limited in their awareness of God's inner wisdom, truth and eternal realities. They based their observations only on physical phenomenon and the physical world. They did not accept invisible planes of reality. They were not aware of higher dimensions. God's divine plan did not exist in their minds. However, they accepted consciousness as having a conscience. They knew there was good and evil which exists in the world.

Existentialism limits the mind to outer actions and worldly happenings. Existence is all there is to depend on in facing daily life and problems. Existentialists do not pray to God or ask God for guidance to solve their daily needs and problems. They reason out their problems to solve problems and issues. They resolve their emotional responses by thinking how to resolve their reactions and problems. All existence is based on how to survive and to face human realities. Many existentialists may be moral even if they don't believe in God.

Existentialism has been a well known philosophy over sixty years. College students study existentialism in philosophy classes as well as to read about other, Western philosophies.

—— TWENTY-SIX ——

WEEKEND ADVENTURES

Weekends are a time to relax and to experience adventures. We look forward to different and exciting experiences when we have at least two days to enjoy ourselves. We plan in advance so we can have fun and amusement during our free time.

There are many interesting things we can do on weekends such as hiking, strolling, fishing, swimming, skating, roller derby, boating, surfing, snorkeling, diving, play tennis, volleyball, basketball, football and kickball, etc. A person can go to the recreational centers such as Disneyland, Knottsberry Farm, the Wax Museum and Balboa Park in San Diego. Eating out at different restaurants, cafes and fast food places are other things to do.

It is an adventure to walk on beaches. You can walk in the ocean as well as pick up dry kelp, shells and rocks. You can sun bathe on the beach. You can prepare picnic and barbecue wieners, hamburgers and steaks on the beach, at campgrounds and in one's backyard. It is fun to get together for outings with relatives, friends and school acquaintances.

Special celebrations take place usually on holiday weekends such as Labor Day weekend, the Fourth of July, Thanksgiving, Christmas and Easter. People get together for parties, festivals, carnivals and they even attend County Fairs and the Circus. All these events are exciting and fun.

So, enjoy weekend adventures. Pick and chose what you want to do. There are many indoor and outdoor events to appreciate especially on weekends.

— TWENTY-SEVEN —

LEARNING TO READ

Learning to read is necessary so we can learn to comprehend what has been written in books, magazines, newspapers, billboards and signs, etc. We have learned to speak in our native language first from early childhood on.

Reading skills have been developed in primary school and throughout elementary school and even in high school. Phonics is learned after children learn the alphabet. Children learn to sound out vowels and consonants. Vowels are a, e, i, o, u and sometimes y. Consonants are b, c, d, f, g, h, j, k, l, m, n, p, q, r, s, t, v, w, x, y and z.

Beginning, initial sounds of the first letter in words are pronounced. Then vowel sounds in the words are pronounced. The word ending is pronounced. Rhyming words are learned from charts and name cards such as at, bat, cat, hat, mat, pat, rat, sat and tat. Many rhyming word lists can be used so children can learn to recognize many rhyming words.

Reading begins by recognizing words in very simple sentences. Sentences are repeated again and again. Eventually, children learn more and more words which they are able to recognize as they read books.

Spelling words presented once a week help to increase one's vocabulary. Each list of words are to be learned and spelled correctly. These words are put in sentences. Spelling exercises are answered in spelling books each week in school. The spelling exercises are about the list of words. Certain grammar is learned step by step with each word list. Usually fifteen or more words are presented each week. Within five or six years a person has an opportunity to learn hundreds of words to add to their vocabulary.

By the time a person is 12 years old he or she has learned thousands of words which he or she can read. Individuals are able to recognize many words which he or she has learned to pronounce and spell properly. Individuals are able to read a variety of books because he or she has a good vocabulary. Individuals continue to learn new vocabulary as they continue to read more books.

Leaning to read is important. We learn many ideas and facts by reading many books. We need to learn the meaning of words so we can comprehend what we read. Reading comprehension is very important so we can understand whatever we read.

── TWENTY-EIGHT ──

PUZZLEMENTS AND PREDICAMENTS

Puzzlements occur when a person is confused and amazed about certain experiences. A person can experience a variety of predicaments. Predicaments are problems which have not been resolved. A person can become overwhelmed with one problem after another. He or she does not know how to resolve certain serious problems.

Joel McLeish was a chemist in a laboratory. He was trying to discover a new, healing serum and anti-biotic to cure certain rare forms of cancer. Radiation treatments generally are given to patients with certain types of cancer. Joel McLeish had spent many years studying Chemistry and Biology. He felt puzzled by the many types of cancer in which there are cures.

The chemistry laboratory where Joel McLeish worked contained many lab tables and stored chemistry equipment. Test tubes and microscopes were available at many tables. Chemistry cabinets were supplied with many chemistry items needed to do lab work. Joel took specimens of laboratory bacteria and cancer cells to observe and study under the microscopes. He learned to examine different cancer tissues carefully.

Joel McLeish hoped to discover cures for breast cancer, colon cancer and lymph cancer. He wanted to find a way to prevent cancer cells from developing. He also wanted to find ways to develop cancer cells from spreading. Joel worked many hours during regular work days to find specific cures for rare cancers. He wanted to save the lives of many people.

Different patients had samples of their cancer tissue sent to the chemistry laboratory to be carefully examined and studied. He developed certain serum formulas to inject in different cancer patients. He wanted to find out if the new serum formulas would work and take affect in volunteer patients when the new serums didn't stop cancer cells from spreading.

Joel felt that his new serums should succeed in preventing cancer and future cancer cells from occurring. Joel had experimented on guinea pigs and rats. Why didn't this new serum cure people? Joel was very puzzled and perplexed about why the new serum was not taking effect in human beings. He was very distressed and disappointed about this especially when he worked so hard to strengthen the new serum. He realized that human beings would need a much stronger dose of the new serum to be cured of different kinds of cancers. The predicament was to determine how much more serum was needed to be effective.

Jack kept experimenting to find more effective ways to create an effective serum to cure rare cancers. He would need enough government funds in order to pay for the needed equipment and serum to cover the necessary costs. He applied for government grants to pay for the lab work and observations. The problem was that the government lacked enough financial aid.

Joel wanted to cover his medical research no matter if he needed financial assistance. He didn't want to give up his mission to find adequate cures for rare cancers. It was a puzzlement why Joel had to struggle to obtain the necessary financial aid for his worthy endeavor to discover a medical breakthrough to cure different cancers.

Joel continued to work in his chemistry laboratory to discover more effective serums despite his limited financial aid. He was determined to succeed in his endeavor to discover effective, new serums and antibiotics. He vaccinated volunteers to find out what results took place. He figured that if a cure had taken place for malaria and polio, he would be able to find effective cures for cancers.

After vaccinating hundreds of volunteers Joel was able to find an effective cure for rare cancers. He was excited about his breakthrough in discovering ways to cure many people of rare cancers.

—— TWENTY-NINE ——

THE ENCHANTING GARDEN

An enchanting garden is an ideal place for fairies and angels to dwell. Sparkling, diamond light shines on many flowers and leaves which continue to glitter magically. Fairies fly around among the trees, flowers and grass. Fairies dance on large, flower petals. They sing celestial melodies as they dance. They are happy to sing of the beauty of the golden, purple, orange and pink flowers growing immensely near a magical forest of verdant, sparkling, silver pine and spruce trees.

This enchanting garden was a peaceful , harmonious abode for many celestial fairies and angels. The fairies and angels dazzled with light as they fluttered their wings. They were the size of tulip flowers. Birds chirped as they perched on the flowers. Bees buzzed as they searched for pollen. Ants moved on the garden floor looking for food. The flowers swayed in the wind and sang celestial harmonies. The fairies and angels communicated with the flowers. Many flowers had star designs. They beamed with rays of light. Angels and fairies continued to mingle among singing flowers. They became friends with the flower and tree kingdom. Fairies and angels felt blissful and uplifted in the magnificent, enchanting garden of roses, tulips, lilies, daisies, pansies and daffodils.

Fairies and angels dwelled in the enchanting garden for many years in harmony. They were protected, so they were safe and tranquil. When it rained, drops of water came down on the flowers, grass and trees. Dewdrops sparkled on the leaves and flowers.

Flowers, trees and grass emanated a pleasant fragrance. This pleasant fragrance permeated in the enchanting garden, forest of trees and surrounding area. This enchanting garden was a heavenly paradise. The fairies drank dewdrops which were on flower petals and broad leaf leaves.

Angels sprinkled sparkling light on all the growing flowers, verdant leaves and majestic trees. This sparkling light lit up the enchanting garden and nearby forest.

The fairies and angels expected to live in the enchanting garden forever. They did not foresee any negative changes in the future. They continued to exist in a peaceful, blissful environment.

Then one day a raging storm occurred in the valley where the enchanting garden and forest existed. The storm was very fierce, causing severe wind, torrent and heavy rainfall. The angels stayed in the trees to protect the fairies from the strong gusts of wind.

The fierce wind darkened the sky. The sparkling light disappeared because the sky was dark for quite some time. The storm continued for several days and nights. The enchanted garden was covered with water. The beautiful flowers were covered with rain water. They no longer sparkled and they no longer emanated a pleasant fragrance. They were covered entirely with water so they no longer sang celestial harmonies. The flowers floated in the water.

The fairies hoped the heavy storm would go away. They waited in the forest in the tall tree branches and hollow trunks for the fierce wind and the heavy rain to stop. Finally, after five days the wind slowed down and the rain stopped. The sun began to shine again. The enchanted garden was still covered with water, which had risen at least six feet high.

It took several months for the rain water to evaporate. When the flood had drained and flowed away, the enchanted garden could be seen again. It didn't look the same because the flowers were affected by the heavy flood. It would take time before the enchanted garden was restored to its former beauty. The fairies and angels flew out of the silver pine trees to look around in the valley where the enchanted garden once existed. The fairies and angels hoped the enchanted garden would be restored. They moved around awaiting for the flowers to reappear and green grass to spread across the valley.

Within six months the bright, colorful flowers began to bloom again. The new flowers sparkled and were lit up by the sunshine. Verdant grass began to grow. The fairies and angels flew back into the new, enchanted garden. They began singing celestial melodies as they moved among the fragrant, colorful flowers. They were happy to be back in the enchanted garden again.

— THIRTY —

FASCINATING SHELLS

Fascinating shells wash up on many beaches from the ocean. The nautilus shell with its spiraling shape and light magenta-brown and white designs stands out. The sound of the ocean can be heard, coming from inner chambers of the nautilus shell.

Giant clam shells lie at the bottom of the deep blue ocean. Giant clams open their enormous shells while they are living. Giant clam shells can be used to make miniature sinks in tree houses.

Sand dollars have interesting designs. Scallop shells have curved designs. They are very artistic. Peewee shells, smaller clam shells and periwinkle shells appear unique. The conch shell has an unusual shape. Conch shells have been used to blow into to alert Polynesian people of ceremonies and other special occasions.

Clams are gathered in the ocean near the shore in the wet sand. Clam shovels are used to dig up clams. They should be at least twelve inches wide before they are used for food.

Abalone shells are very useful because of their myriad colors. If abalone shells are polished the fascinating colors shine beautifully. Abalone shells are displayed on shelves and tables as special decoration.

Many sea shells make fascinating displays in your home and garden. A variety of shells add a natural look around your home and garden.

THIRTY-ONE

EDUCATED PEOPLE

Educated people generally have a well rounded awareness of books, ideas, places, cultures and people. Educated people learn to comprehend many concepts, viewpoints, opinions, facts and figures. An educated person learns that many options and solutions exist. They tend to be more flexible and they understand issues and problems better because of their awareness of specific knowledge.

Generally an educated person receives a bachelor's degree, a master's degree and even a Ph.D. in specific fields of study. He or she learns to write essays, reports, theses and documentaries. An educated person usually processes research papers on computers.

To become educated a person goes to college libraries, public libraries and library firms to look up research in encyclopedias, reference books and author's books about given topics and issues. A person can learn a lot about many subjects and topics. Detailed information is available in research books.

An educated person is capable of reading well and understanding many ideas, examples, illustrations and diagrams in a variety of technical books. He or she learns to express many ideas and facts about different subjects.

An educated person should present speeches and participate in debates and in intelligent discussions. To express creative ideas and to use one's imagination is important. An educated person usually is able to communicate effectively. He or she is usually well groomed and he or she dresses appropriately for every occasion.

An educated person usually adapts well in most situations. He or she uses reasoning and problem solving methods to resolve issues and problems. An educated person usually adjusts better because he or she experiences more balance and understanding about life.

THIRTY-TWO

BIRDS OF THE WORLD

Millions of birds live in the world in different locations. Some birds live only in the Northern Hemisphere. Some birds live below the equator in the Southern Hemisphere. Many birds migrate during different seasons. They migrate south to warmer climates when it gets too cold to stay where they were. Many birds have difficulty living in very cold climates. Birds usually live in flocks.

Birds, which live in the Northern Hemisphere above the equator, are robins, blackbirds, whippoorwills, sparrows, cormorants, geese, seagulls, herons, quails, peacocks, doves, blue jays, meadowlarks, woodpeckers, nightingales, owls, humming birds, mud hens, turkeys, roosters, chickens, red-breasted robins, puffins, shags, eagles, hawks and wrens. They adapt to colder climates. They usually build nests with twigs, brush and sticks in trees and bushes. They lay eggs usually during the springtime. They migrate as soon as the climate is too cold to warmer places.

Birds which live in the Southern Hemisphere are kiwis, vultures, flamingos, roosters, chickens, cranes, parrots, cockatoos, parakeets, pelicans, storks and seagulls. Peacocks and doves also live in the tropics. Scavengers usually live in warm climates. However, they have been seen in colder climates. They eat the remains of carcasses as well as garbage and leftovers.

Thousands of pink flamingos flock together in harbors in the tropics. They have long necks and pink feathers. Peacocks display their beautiful, colorful plumes as they strut by.

Eagles, hawks, storks, puffins and shags build large nests on high cliffs and ledges. They must leave the nest to hunt for food to bring back to their young in the high nests on the cliffs and high ledges. The young birds must learn to fly out of the high nests as they learn to fly.

Seagulls, pelicans, roosters and chickens live up in the Northern Hemisphere and Southern Hemisphere. Brolgas are Australian birds which are built like an ostrich. It has a long, thin neck with a crimson colored head. Gibberbirds are found in the National Park in South Australia. Black swans live in Western Australia.

Owls sleep during the day and are awake at night. They build their nests in high trees. They hunt for food during the night. Owls make hooting sounds. They have big, piercing, bright eyes.

Eagles and hawks fly high and swoop down quickly to pick up their prey with their sharp claws. They also have sharp beaks which they use to eat food.

Seagulls dwell on beaches and lagoons both in the Northern and Southern Hemispheres. They survive in both warm and cold climates. Seagulls are seen on many beaches and lagoons in California even during the winter months. They adapt to cold climates.

Pelicans flock together by hundreds and they dwell on large, flat cliffs together. They protect their young pelicans that remain on the cliffs until they learn to fly with the pelican flocks. Pelicans live in the Northern and Southern Hemispheres. They adapt to cooler climates. If it becomes too cold pelicans migrate to warmer climates in the south.

All birds hatch from egg shells. Birds are not mammals. They may migrate to warmer climates to survive better. They can find more food usually in warmer climates. Some birds must travel to warmer climates in order to stay alive. Birds eat insects, seeds and scraps. They usually build nests to lay eggs in. Birds have existed on Earth for millions of years. They may continue to exist for many years.

THIRTY-THREE

LIFE IN NEW ZEALAND

New Zealand consists of islands near Australia in the Southern Hemisphere below the equator in the Pacific Ocean. Wellington is the capital city. New Zealand is susceptible to many earthquakes. New Zealand is made up of three islands.

Wellington is located in the southern location of the northern island. It is the largest city in New Zealand. There are museums, art galleries, beautiful parks and the University of New Zealand. Many cultural events occur in Wellington.

Auckland is the second largest city in New Zealand. The University of New Zealand is an educational institution in Auckland.

The Maoris are a Polynesian group of natives who have lived in New Zealand for thousands of years. They carved wooden, pagan ideals and build unique houses with carved wooden designs around the edges of their Maori houses. Maori women wear tappa cloth outfits. They throw long strings with white balls on the end of each string. Maori women throw the long strings with balls up in the air.

New Zealand is known for its redwood forests which have grown on New Zealand for thousands of years. New Zealanders raise sheep and cattle. They grow fruits and vegetables in many valleys and on farmland.

The Maoris have maintained their cultural traditions. They still perform ancient dances and dress in native costumes. They sing Maori songs and believe in nature spirits and gods. They worship the sun gods, rain gods and fire gods.

Maori men stuck out their tongues to scare away enemies. They performed fierce dances using spears. The Maori people were fierce warriors. They painted their faces to look fierce. Maori warriors fought battles with invaders who came to New Zealand for many centuries.

Today, New Zealand has become progressive islands with a Democratic government. A woman, Helen Clark, became the leader of the government. She promoted peace and a better economy. Tourists visit New Zealand, which is another way the economy thrives. Tourism has become a major industry.

Tourists can observe a variety of landscapes and climates in New Zealand. Eggs can be cooked on hot rocks. Geysers burst up through blow holes along the coast near Christchurch on the southern island. Mount Cook is the only mountain. Tourists can see snow on

Mount Cook. Christchurch is an interesting historical place with old, historical buildings.

There are a variety of things to do in New Zealand. Tourists and New Zealanders can go boating, snorkeling, fishing, horseback riding, surfing, sailing, windsurfing, whitewater rafting and see historical museums and cultural centers showing ancient Maori customs and beliefs. New Zealand has verdant, green valleys, a majestic mountain and scenic coastal and ocean views. The climate is usually pleasant with many sunny days.

——— THIRTY-FOUR ———

BEACH ADVENTURES

Beaches are wonderful places to explore bays, coastal locations and enjoy warm sands. Many beaches have shells, kelp and driftwood. Seagulls and pelicans dwell on many beaches.

Angela and Warren Wilcox decided to walk on a long beach on the Gold Coast of Australia near Brisbane. The Gold Coast is a long beach of many miles. The pristine sand is warmer in the hot, summer sun.

Angela and Warren walked in the warm sand in their bare feet. They cooled their feet in the ocean. They allowed ocean waves to cool their feet. The cool ocean waves continued to sooth their feet. They walked for miles on this pristine beach. They observed boats moving in the ocean. The beautiful, turquoise, blue was very magnificent to view. White, rippling waves swept to shore. Many high waves crashed in the ocean and rolled to the shore.

Angela and Warren continued to walk south on the Gold Coast beach. They stopped there to collect interesting shells. They gathered shells in a cloth sack. They gathered periwinkles, conch shells and sand dollars. They decided to rest on the beach sand after walking three miles because they were tired. So, they laid down on the warm sand to rest. It took time to recover from their long walk.

It began to become dark. Angela and Warren were so far down the beach to the south they depended on each other to get back to civilization. They decided to stay on the beach overnight because it was a moonless night. It was very dark on the sandy beach.

Angela and Warren wrapped up in beach towels and laid down on the warm sand. During the night the sun had gone over the horizon. The air had become much cooler and the beach sand cooled off. Angela and Warren became chilly from the cooler air. During the night sand fleas bit Angela and Warren. They felt the bites of the sand fleas. They were uncomfortable when they woke up the next morning. Red bumps covered their arms and legs.

Warren and Angela witnessed a beautiful sunrise of bright orange, red and yellow colors in the sky as the sun gradually came up over the horizon. They sat up and looked toward the horizon. They enjoyed watching the sunrise.

Angela and Warren started walking north back to Surfers Paradise. They were hungry because they had not eaten for over 14 hours. They had a long walk back along the beach. They carried their cloth sack of shells and they had wrapped their beach towels around their shoulders to keep from getting badly sunburned.

Seagulls and pelicans flew by in flocks. Some seagulls hovered over their heads. Pelicans were darting in the ocean for fish. Some seagulls were resting on the beach. The sun continued to move across the sky.

Warren and Angela walked in the wet sand close to the ocean to keep their feet cooler. The sun began to become hot and piercing. Angela and Warren felt the heat of the sun on their arms, legs and backs. They kept walking despite the rising heat. It would take hours to return to the place they started from.

Finally, after several hours of walking on the long, pristine beach they finally came back to the location they started from. There was a beach café nearby. Warren and Angela walked into the café nearby and ordered some food. Angela ordered scrambled eggs, hash browns, toast, orange juice and coffee. Warren ordered scrambled eggs, waffles, country potatoes, cranberry juice and coffee.

Angela and Warren were eager to eat their food when it arrived at their table. They ate up their food and drank their juice and they sipped their coffee. They were glad to be indoors resting at a table after walking for many miles on the Gold Coast beach.

——— THIRTY-FIVE ———

KEEPING SECRETS

People keep secrets because they don't want other people to know certain experiences and problems they know about. Secrets may not be revealed for many years. Once a secret is revealed it is out in the open. People react when secrets are revealed to them.

Thelma Johnson was a conservative, secretive person. She was 32 years old and she was still unmarried. Thelma kept certain things a secret that had happened to her that she felt were embarrassing and too awful to tell anyone else about..

Thelma had dated different men when she was in her twenties. She had dated a man, who was very assertive. She finally surrendered herself to him. He made love over and over to her out of wedlock. Thelma became pregnant because she was not taking birth control pills or wearing any birth control protection. She was pregnant when she was twenty-two years old. Thelma kept her pregnancy secret from her parents, friends and even the fellow who impregnated her. She didn't want to marry him.

When Thelma was three months pregnant she decided to have her pregnancy terminated. She went to someone who knew how to perform an abortion. She saved enough money to pay for the abortion. She went into a private room at the abortionist home so he could perform the abortion. She felt badly about having the abortion. Yet, she went through with it.

Once the abortion was performed, Thelma had to recover from the surgical procedure. She bled for a period of time. She was in severe pain for several months after the abortion. Yet, she didn't tell anyone about the abortion

Several years went by and Thelma continued to keep the abortion a secret. She continued to date different men. She decided to be fitted for a protective device so she wouldn't get pregnant out of wedlock. Thelma continued to experience sexual intercourse out of wedlock. She didn't get pregnant. She was an attractive woman.

Finally, Thelma met a man she wanted to marry when she was 32 years old. He was very compatible, healthy, pleasant and attractive. She fell in love with him instantly. His name was Lockwood Atherton. Lockwood was a successful architect. He was 34 years old.

Thelma continued to keep her secret about her abortion when she was twenty-two. She still felt badly about making this decision to abort a fetus. She didn't want

Lockwood to know that she had slept with other men out of wedlock. She kept it a secret about her various affairs with men.

Thelma wanted to get married to Lockwood Atherton. She waited for him to ask her to marry him. After they dated for approximately one year, Lockwood finally asked Thelma to marry him. Thelma naturally said yes to his proposal. She was very happy to have the opportunity to get married at last.

Lockwood and Thelma were married that Spring in May. Thelma wore a beautiful, long white dress to the wedding. Lockwood wore an attractive blue suit with a ruffled white shirt and white bow-tie and leather shoes.

After the wedding ceremony there was a wedding reception. Lockwood and Thelma cut the wedding cake. They received many wedding presents. They went on their honeymoon to a remote place in the Virgin Islands. They spent two weeks enjoying this tropical location. When they came back to their new home they went on with their lives.

Lockwood continued to work as an architect. Thelma had become a nurse. She worked at a local, doctor's clinic near her new home. After a period of years she became pregnant. This time Thelma intended to keep her baby.

During Thelma's pregnancy she had some complications. She began spotting with blood. Finally, she lost the baby because she had a miscarriage. Thelma and

Lockwood were both upset about Thelma's miscarriage. She was 34 years old.

Thelma waited nearly six months before she tried to have another baby. She became pregnant again. When she was approximately three months pregnant she had another miscarriage. Thelma was beside herself with grief over the second miscarriage. She was warned that she wouldn't be able to have a baby. So, she went to a baby specialist to be examined. He examined her female parts carefully. He even took X-rays. He told her that the area in the vagina near the womb opening had been cut in such a manner so she could not have a full term pregnancy.

The doctor asked Thelma if she had ever had an abortion. Thelma broke down and cried. She didn't want to tell the doctor about her abortion when she was twenty-two. She hoped to keep this secret from him. She finally revealed that she had an abortion. The doctor said that whoever performed the abortion did a very poor job which caused Thelma to miscarry any baby she would have in the future.

Thelma left the doctor's office feeling deep regret that she had an abortion years ago. She didn't want to tell her husband about the abortion. She still decided to keep the abortion she had when she was twenty-two a secret. She was too embarrassed and humiliated to tell him about it.

Thelma was unable to have a full term pregnancy. Lockwood wanted children. So, Lockwood and Thelma adopted two toddlers. They adopted a girl and a boy. Thelma never told Lockwood why she couldn't have a full-term pregnancy.

THIRTY-SIX

BETTY HUTTON'S LIFE

Betty Hutton became an actress in her early twenties. She went to Hollywood and eventually acted in small parts in different films. In time, she was selected to act in Perils of PERILS OF PAULINE. She performed stunts, danced on stages and sang love songs. She also was chosen to act a major roll in THE GREATEST SHOW ON EARTH. Betty Hutton performed difficult acrobatic stunts on trapeze wires. She was vivacious and very attractive.

Betty Hutton married and had several children. However, she was very busy acting in different films. She had little time to spend with her children. She was divorced several times.

Betty Hutton was interviewed by Robert Osborne, who is a host for Turner Classic Movies. Betty revealed that she found peace and spiritual awareness when she retired from acting. She attended the Catholic Church. She was given spiritual guidance by a priest of the Catholic Church. He advised Betty to become close to

Jesus Christ as her Lord and savior. Betty did volunteer work at the Catholic Church. She told Robert Osborne that her new, spiritual life was far more fulfilling than her lifestyle as a movie star in Hollywood. Betty Hutton lived to the age of 105.

—— THIRTY-SEVEN ——

HEALING CONSCIOUSNESS

THE HEALING CONSCIOUSNESS, A DOCTOR'S JOURNEY TO HEALING was written by Beth Baughman DuPree, M.D. in 2006. Beth Baughman DuPree helped establish the Healing Consciousness Foundation which provides funding for the services that standard health care does not cover but are vitally needed by women, men and their families when faced with a breast cancer diagnosis. This healing foundation empowers women and men with breast cancer to find healing emotionally, physically and spiritually. This healing center is located at 3300 Tillman Drive, Bensalem, Pennsylvania. The phone number is 1-215-633-3450. The email address is www.hcfbucks.org

Beth Baughman DuPree has stated that, "the healing consciousness is awareness found deep within ourselves, where we embrace the eternal nature of our souls and release all fear of death. Embracing this awareness, we are free to embrace the present moment fully. Illness and diseases teach us to embrace the moment and live the journey to the fullest for no one is guaranteed tomorrow." Dr. DuPree suggests that we should live to the fullest because we never know how long we will live on Earth.

Dr. Beth DuPree has stated, "the art of healing has been lost by the technologically advanced society we have embraced." She said, "historically masculine energy developed medical technology with all its wonders. Feminine energy focuses on the mind, body and spiritual connection, embracing a concept of healing that includes more than curing diseases."

Dr. Beth Dupree has performed surgery on thousands of patients. The personal and energetic connection she shares with her patients is as important as their healing process as to the surgery she performs. Her focus as a physician has shifted from one based solely on Western medicine to one that combines the wisdom of Eastern medicine with state of the art Western medical technology.

Beth was born and raised in York, Pennsylvania and is the youngest of seven children. She is a graduate of the University of Pittsburg and Hahmemorn University School of Medicine. She completed her surgical residency at Albert Einstein Medical Center in Philadelphia. Dr. Beth DuPree has practiced surgery in Buck's County, Pennsylvania since 1992. She specializes in the diagnosis and treatment of diseases of the breast.

Beth lives with her husband Joe and their sons Tom and Dean.

Beth DuPree's mother-in-law's employer, a surgeon, was a believer in past life regression and therefore reincarnation. Beth Dupre stated, "a breast with cancer can be removed and reconstructed. Women do not die of cancer in their breasts. They die when the disease spreads outside of the breast. There are women who do not obtain screening mammography out of fear that they might have cancer. To me the fear lies in having cancer that is not found. If you do not look for cancer it does not mean that it does not exist. It just means you chose to ignore its presence. Early detection of cancer leads to less invasive treatments and a greater likelihood of cure."

Dr. Beth DuPree has stated, "knowledge is empowering and fear paralyzes. We wanted to educate women about the choices they have when it comes to caring for their breasts. We were the pebble in the pond whose ripple effect would expand far wider than we had ever imagined. Years later many people still comment on the impact of the event. Beth realized she was able to save the lives of many women who had breast cancer. She recalled her father's voice saying, "The only limits you have in your life are those you place upon yourself." Beth realized that she had no limits.

In January of 2000 Beth reached a point in her career that required a major change. She decided not to continue simply as a general surgeon. She knew that she needed to do more than just operate on people. Beth began to focus on holism. Holism is the basis for treatment of disease in Eastern Medicine. Multiple systems must be evaluated because they relate to one another rather than existing as individual components. The whole is greater than the sum of the parts. Holistic care includes evaluation and treatment of the physical, mental and spiritual components of an individual, not just a person's physical symptoms. All three are completely interconnected and intertwined. Beth DuPree has continued to apply the holistic approach to healing. She has healed many women who had breast cancer.

THIRTY-EIGHT

BECOMING SELF PUBLISHED

Becoming self-published requires different steps. First, you must write an original poetry, plays fiction and nonfiction manuscripts. The manuscripts must be typed properly in a specific format. Your original, typed manuscript must have a copyright from the Library of Congress Copyright Office in Washington D.C.

You need to create a publishing company. It is too expensive to print books because of the cost of printing equipment. You can have a printing company in your local area print your manuscript to produce books. You should mention your publishing company name and the date your book was published.

Once you have submitted a copy of your book you must wait for the copyright papers to be sent to you. The copyright number should be typed in the copyright section of your book. Copyright is necessary so nobody can claim the specific ideas in your book.

After you have become self published you should be sure to distribute your books to different book stores so perspective customers can purchase your books. You should keep at least one copy of your published books.

You need to advertise about your book in newspapers, magazines and bulletins. List your book or books on the Internet. You should write a synopsis about your book and a biography about yourself. A 2 inch by 2 inch photo of yourself can be put on the back cover of your book. Ask the printer to design an artistic, interesting front cover.

Becoming self published is worthwhile as well as an exciting experience.

—— THIRTY-NINE ——

SUMMER CRUISE

Taking cruises across the ocean can be a wonderful experience. You can enjoy brilliant sunsets and captivating sunrises. Many views of the ocean are quite worthwhile. White ripples can be seen in the distance. The moon and stars come out at night. The moon can be seen over the horizon with the bright light reflected from the sun. Ocean water moves to and fro and rolls against the cruise ship. The deep blue sea can be seen for many miles to the horizon.

Cruise ships carry many passengers who are tourists traveling across the ocean to a certain location for a vacation. Tourists go on cruise ships to Polynesian islands, to the Mediterranean Sea to European countries and islands. Some cruises are taken to Alaska and the Bering Straits. Other cruises are taken to Mexico.

Nora Miller, who was 32, was an elementary school teacher. She enjoyed traveling during summertime when she had nearly three months of free time. She planned to take a cruise to Europe in June. She would travel through the summer months. She lived in Los Angeles, California and taught elementary school there.

In June, Nora packed several suitcases. She boarded a large cruise ship in Los Angeles Harbor. She shared a ship cabin with another lady passenger. She had a view from the cabin terrace and deck. She unpacked her clothes and put them away in a closet close to her bed.

Once Nora was settled in her ship cabin she dressed in comfortable clothes and shoes. She decided to walk around the passenger ship. She walked up to the main deck to look around. She saw dolphins swimming in the ocean in schools near the cruise ship. She walked by a big swimming pool and then she came to a miniature golf course in another section. Passengers of all age groups were strolling around on the top deck dressed casually.

Nora noticed an outdoor snack bar near the swimming pool. She decided to stroll over to this snack bar. She sat at an outdoor table with a veranda-umbrella which provided shade. Nora also noticed there were many, single women browsing near the swimming pool and some of the women were sitting at the table at snack bars. They were dressed in swimsuits and bikinis.

Nora decided to sit at a table near the swimming pool. She observed passengers swimming in the pool. Some passengers were diving off the diving board. Some passengers were enjoying drinks and eating snacks at the snack bar. Everyone appeared to be having a good time. A server came over to Nora's table to take her order. Nora ordered a seven-up and pretzels.

The server went back to the counter to prepare the order. He came back within five minutes with a seven-up in a glass of ice. He also had a sack of pretzels on the tray with the cold drink. He served the seven-up and pretzels to Nora. She paid the server for the seven-up and pretzels.

Nora began sipping the seven-up. She munched some pretzels. She continued to look around at what was happening around her. She felt relaxed and happy to be on a cruise to Europe. She had looked forward to this cruise for many months.

Once Nora had finished enjoying her snack she decided to go swimming in the big, nearby pool. She took off her blouse. She took off her shoes. She put on a swimsuit. Then she jumped into the warm, swimming pool. She swam around in the deep end of the pool. Other people were splashing water and kicking their feet in the pool. Nora swam across the long pool to exercise. She did some breast strokes and back strokes.

Nora remained in the swimming pool for at least an hour. Then she came out of the pool. She dried off with a towel. She sat in a deck chair near the pool to sun herself. She relaxed near the pool for at least another hour. Then she walked back to her room on the ship and changed into regular clothes.

It was time for lunch. So, Nora headed for the ship's restaurant to enjoy fish, chips and cole slaw. She also sipped some ice with lemon. She sat at a table for six people. Other passengers sat at her table. Nora introduced herself to these passengers. There were three women and two men who sat at her table.

Nora was attracted to the younger man who appeared to be around thirty-eight. He had red hair and clear, blue eyes. He was tall, strong looking and slender. He introduced himself. He said, "Hello. My name is Jorge. What is your name?" Nora replied, "My name is Nora. Are you planning to go to Europe?" Jorge answered, "Yes, I'm going to the Mediterranean Sea to coastal cities and harbors. Where are you headed?" Nora replied, "I am going to the Mediterranean Sea, too. We should be there within a week." Jorge smiled warmly at Nora. He observed that she had strawberry, blonde hair, which hung down her neck, and blue eyes. She was well built and dressed in a casual outfit with tennis shoes on. Nora was approximately five feet six inches tall.

Jorge was attracted to Nora immediately because she was very attractive and seemed interesting to know. He continued visiting with her while they ate their dinners. Jorge revealed that he was a college professor of History and Semantics. He was on leave of absence for one year. So, he decided to travel around the world to different, scenic locations. He was taking photographs and producing videos of his traveling experiences.

Nora found out that Jorge had written and published several travel books. His books were circulated around the world at many book stores. Jorge Wright was a well known author. He was a successful professor of History of Semantics.

Nora was impressed with Jorge's accomplishments. During the cruise to the Mediterranean Sea Nora became acquainted with Jorge. They often strolled around the cruise ship together. They played miniature golf, table tennis and they went to the exercise room together. They shared different meals during the voyage.

When Nora went to her cabin at night she sat out on the terrace balcony attached to her cabin. She observed the moon over the ocean. Her cabin mate slept in a different bed nearby. Her roommate was in her fifties. This was the first cruise she had ever taken. She was a widow. Her name was Tillie Smothers. Nora became acquainted with her roommate, Tillie during the two weeks the cruise ship was traveling to Europe near the Mediterranean Sea.

The cruise ship finally arrived in the Mediterranean Sea. Marseilles was the first destination. Nora and Jorge left the cruise ship to tour around the exotic, cultural resort of Marseilles. They went to museums, art galleries, cafes and stores. They enjoyed French food in a Marseilles restaurant. The art galleries had a variety of paintings and artifacts worth seeing.

During the evening Nora and Jorge went dancing at a club in Marseilles. They walked on the cobblestone streets in the moonlight. They returned to the cruise ship late at night. Nora was tempted to stay the rest of the night in Jorge's cabin. At the last minute she changed her mind. Jorge had not totally committed himself to her yet. She decided to not go too far until she was sure Jorge was serious about her. She was not promiscuous. She wanted to be loved and needed before she became intimate.

The cruise ship continued on to Naples in Italy. This popular port city had a magnificent, seafront harbor. The ocean was a turquoise-blue color which was very picturesque. Nora visited the famous underwater cave at the Isle of Capri. She witnessed crystal clear water with white sand on the seafloor. This was a very special place. She sat in a rowboat and looked down into the crystal blue water.

The cruise ship continued on to Athens, a well known Greek city. Athens is the capital of Greece. Greek gods are displayed with large, stone statues. The Greeks have outdoor theaters. Jorge and Nora toured some Greek temples and attended an amphitheater. They saw an outdoor Greek play which was a tear jerker. They walked among Greek ruins. Stone, majestic columns were visible everywhere.

Barcelona was a charming Spanish city with red tiled terraced roofs and thick stucco homes and other buildings. Nora and Jorge ate at an outdoor patio on a terrace overlooking the ocean. By now, Jorge had become serious about Nora. They had spent nearly two months together. Nora finally became intimate with Jorge because he asked her to marry him. Nora was very happy to meet the man of her dreams.

The cruise ship stopped at Crete which was a historical island with traditional villages and interesting, spicy food. Nora and Jorge continued on to Sicily. The ocean views were colorful and blissful to observe.

The Mediterranean Sea was much larger than Nora thought. She was enjoying many Mediterranean views, seaports and outdoor cafes. She enjoyed many Mediterranean dishes. Jorge introduced Nora to quality red and white wines. He knew a lot about wines and different, European dishes. Jorge was a cosmopolitan person.

After the cruise ship had stopped at different Mediterranean seaports and cities the ship headed across the ocean back to Los Angeles Harbor along the southern coast of California. Jorge lived in La Jolla, California. La Jolla is approximately one hundred miles south of Los Angeles.

Jorge continued to date Nora for a period of time. They recalled their romantic and adventurous cruise to the Mediterranean Sea and seaports. They were very glad they had met on this summer cruise. Nora and Jorge were married six months later after they returned from this magnificent cruise to Europe.

—— FORTY ——

DAILY PRAYERS

Daily prayers can be very helpful because when we pray we are asking for spiritual sustenance and guidance. Daily prayers can bring us closer to God and our higher self. The higher self is part of God's spiritual reality. Our soul focuses on spiritual awareness when we pray. Our emotions may be calmed down as we pray for divine protection to help us develop spiritual strength.

Daily prayers help us to awaken to truth and inner peace. Each prayer brings us closer to God. A quiet time in a peaceful setting is a time to reflect on our lives. We need to look within to know and identify with our higher thoughts. We have a Christ Self deep within to realize and know God. Life without God realization can be meaningless because God is the source for our existence. To know God is to know the purpose of life. So, continue to maintain daily prayers to develop spiritual oneness and awareness of life.

You will be happier and spiritually stronger if you pray everyday. You will develop spiritual strength when you develop prayers on a daily basis. Spiritual oneness and strength is important for spiritual development and enfoldment. Spiritual character is established through spiritual discipline and enlightenment day by day, month by month and year by year.

—— FORTY-ONE ——

WHY CERTAIN PEOPLE BECOME RADICALS

Certain people become radicals about certain problems, issues and concerns. A radical person has become extreme in his or her opinions and viewpoints about life. Major issues in the world effect our perceptions and understanding of daily life.

Certain people who become extreme in their opinions and beliefs generally become imbalanced about what they believe in. These individuals may influence many people around them. They want to encourage other people to follow their beliefs and accept their opinions. They may be willing to fight for their extreme convictions. This may bring suffering and grief to others. Radical people continue to maintain strong and even destructive viewpoints.

Radical people may become political and social leaders in the world. They may be very prejudiced and strong willed about what they believe in. As a result, they may bring harm and much danger to masses of people who follow their beliefs. We need to recognize radical thinking and reasoning so we can avoid following radical viewpoints and beliefs.

Adolph Hitler, who was the leader of the Nazi regime, was extremely radical. He believed the Aryan race was superior to everyone. He exterminated six million Jews because he hated them. He told everyone that they were inferior and should not live. He caused World War II to start. He wanted to become a dictator of the world. Hitler harmed many innocent people because of his extremely radical beliefs and actions.

Nero was a Roman emperor who had extremely radical beliefs. He burned Rome down. Then he blamed the early Christians for the burning of Rome. As a result thousands of early Christians were severely punished and killed. Nero also murdered his mother and his wife because he didn't want to accept their beliefs. His wife was pregnant with a future heir to the throne. Nero didn't want any heirs around while he was alive. He was afraid of competition.

Radical people are usually imbalanced because of their perverted opinions. They try to manipulate other people because they want to sway them to believe their radical beliefs. They cause wars to start. They destroy the lives of other people because of their negative influence on others.

It is important to stop extremely radical individuals from coming into political power. Extremely radical individuals should be banned from political influence and control. Masses of people need to be protected from extremely radical individuals.

FORTY-TWO

KNOW YOUR WORLD

We need to learn about our world especially because we live here on Earth. The nature of our planet should be understood. While we attended school we were taught that the Earth is round. The Earth orbits around the Sun. The Earth revolves on its axis every 24 hours. The Earth moves around the Sun in 365 ½ days in a year. The Earth is divided by the equator. There is the Northern Hemisphere and the Southern Hemisphere. The Northern Hemisphere includes Mexico, all of North America, Iceland, Greenland, China, India, Russia, Europe, North Africa, Japan, Asia, many Polynesian Islands, the Middle East and former Soviet republics. Continents below the equator are South America, Southern Africa, Australia and Antarctica. Many Polynesian islands are in the Southern Hemisphere.

There are generally four seasons in the Northern Hemisphere. There is a wet and dry season in the Southern Hemisphere's tropical zones. The tropical zones extend from 23 degrees latitude north and south of the equator. Many tropical zones are hot and humid. However, some are dry deserts like in Peru and part of the Australian Outback, etc. There is snow and sleet in the Northern Hemisphere as well as tropical and desert temperatures in the 90s or 100s F. There is snow in some of the tallest mountains.

We need to learn about landscapes on the surface of the Earth. There are valleys, mountains, jungles, deserts and dense forest areas. When thick clouds form it may rain. When the sky is blue it generally does not rain. Cold weather occurs when the sun is far away from the Earth. The closer the Sun comes to Earth the warmer the Earth's surface is because of the warmth of the Sun's rays. Warm and cold ocean currents also affect land temperatures and rainfall. Coastal Peru is closer to the equator than Hawaii or Tahiti. However, this climate is frequently foggy and chilly due to its cold ocean currents from Antarctica.

We need to learn about the landscapes on the surface of the Earth. There are valleys, mountains, jungles, deserts and dense forest areas. When thick cloud levels form it may rain. When the sky is blue it generally does not rain. Cold weather occurs when the sun is far away from the Earth. The closer the sun's rays come to the Earth the warmer the Earth's surface is because of the warmth of the sun's rays. Warm and cold ocean currents also affect land temperature and rainfall. Coastal Peru is closer to the equator than Hawaii or Tahiti. However, this climate is frequently foggy and chilly due to its cold ocean currents from Antarctica.

We need to take care of our Earth by stopping air, water and earth pollution. We need to avoid manmade, harmful sprays and chemicals plus waste particles from spreading around the Earth. We need to keep the atmosphere clean so we can have clean air to breathe. Land should be kept clean. Waste products can cause pollution in soil. Water pollution is harmful. Polluted water is harmful to drink. Water must be purified and cleansed so it can be used.

By knowing about our Earth we can learn how to protect our planet. We need to take care of our environment. American Indians took care of the Earth. They hunted for food which they used. They didn't waste anything. They didn't cut down too many trees or pollute the streams, lakes and ocean. They conserved their environment.

Modern societies need to learn to conserve trees and use only the food they need. We need to learn not to waste natural resources. We should not chop down too many trees. We should conserve water. We shouldn't waste water. We should take care of our immediate environment on Earth.

Geologists study the topography, climates, flora and fauna and continents on our planet Earth. They observe changes occurring in the tectonic plates inside the Earth. They become aware of many conditions on the

Earth's surface. Oceanographers study the oceans and life deep in the sea. They learn about conditions existing in the ocean. We should continue to learn all we can about the planet Earth.

FORTY-THREE

LEARNING FOREIGN LANGUAGES

Americans should learn to speak and write several foreign languages. Generally, Spanish, French, German and English are valuable foreign languages. English is our native language. Learning to speak and write in Spanish, German and French is useful and worthwhile.

We can communicate effectively with people from Mexico, South America, Germany and Spain if we learn to speak and write in these languages. If you go to Europe it is helpful to learn French and German. Many people speak French in Europe.

Spanish, French and English as well as German are spoken in Europe. Other languages spoken in Scandinavian countries in Europe are Norwegian, Swedish and Finnish. Dutch is spoken in the Netherlands. Most Europeans speak at least three languages.

Conversational methods should be learned. The teacher speaks in the foreign language. Students repeat what the teacher says. Then the teacher translates what he or she repeated. Students learn day by day, step by step how to speak the foreign language. Grammar is introduced such as nouns, verbs, pronouns, adjectives, adverbs and prepositions. Nondescriptive words are also learned. Connection words must be also learned.

Students may be given foreign language textbooks in order to study foreign languages. They are assigned specific exercises about parts of speech. They learn many words which they need to recognize and to read. While students are learning to read new words they are learning to pronounce each new word. These words are put into sentences. One sentence relates to the next sentence because sentences are thoughts which logically express a sequence of thoughts to develop specific paragraphs. Each paragraph has certain ideas in it.

Students can learn to speak and read well in different languages. It takes speaking and repeating different parts of speech in a foreign language to learn that language. Teachers should continue to teach conversational languages. Then more students learn to speak in foreign languages.

In Europe, people are exposed to other people who speak foreign languages. As a result, they begin to learn these languages. They learn to repeat many words. These words are recognized more readily day by day, month by month and year by year. Individuals learn to speak effectively with understanding and comprehension. Teachers can use videos, tapes and records to listen to in order to learn foreign languages. Individuals can repeat what they hear on these listening devices. Constant practice helps a person learn to speak fluently in foreign languages. A person can learn to read well in foreign languages.

—— FORTY-FOUR ——

PRIVATE LIVES OF MOVIE STARS

Movie stars have private lives like most people who are not movie stars. They live in homes which are secluded and usually secured with protective cameras and warning devices. A loud sound goes off if anyone intrudes or invades their home and yards. Movie stars want their privacy as well as to feel safe and comfortable.

Robert Redford lives on a large ranch in a remote area of Utah. He enjoys living like a rancher. He owns horses and cattle. He is accustomed to warm, dry climate. Many movie fans are not aware of Robert Redford's private life. He maintains his privacy and lifestyle.

Joan Crawford lived in a large, three story house with a large garden and a swimming pool. She lived in Bel Air in an elegant home. She adopted two children because she wanted children. She tried to maintain her privacy. Eventually, her adopted children grew up. Her adopted daughter wrote a biography of Joan Crawford a mother who was too strict and that she expected her adopted children to give up their gifts to other less fortunate children. Joan Crawford's life became exposed to the world in a book entitled MOMMY DEAREST. Joan Crawford decided to leave most of her fortune to needy people and institutions. Her adopted children resented their adopted mother for giving away her wealth to other people.

Debbie Reynolds was married several times. She met Eddie Fischer when she was in her early twenties. They were married and they lived in the Los Angeles area in a lovely home. Debbie Reynolds had two children. She was a good mother to her children. Debbie Reynolds had a few happy years of marriage with Eddie Fischer. They were in several movies together.

Eddie Fischer was a popular vocal soloist in the 1950s and 1960s. He met Elizabeth Taylor, who was considered to be the most beautiful woman and famous movie star in the world. Eddie Fischer and Debbie Reynolds were divorced. Eddie Fischer married Elizabeth Taylor. There was a big scandal about Eddie Fischer breaking up with Debbie Reynolds. He lost his popularity because of the scandal. Elizabeth Taylor was considered to be a home wrecker by the world.

Debbie Reynolds eventually met Mr. Karl, a wealthy shoe producer. For awhile he prospered because Karl's shoes were popular. In time, Mr. Karl went bankrupt because he gambled his fortune away in Las Vegas and Reno in Nevada. Debbie Reynolds divorced him and she was broke. She lived in a trailer until she was able to earn enough to move into another nice home.

Debbie Reynolds became a night club singer in a large hotel in Las Vegas. She met her third husband. She became prosperous again. She had paid off some of Mr. Karl's debts when she worked in Las Vegas. Debbie Reynolds had been seen traveling to Hawaii in a public airplane. She was friendly at the Los Angeles International Airport when she was greeted by admirers. Debbie Reynolds continued to act in more Hollywood films.

Elizabeth Taylor was a child movie star from England. She became known in NATIONAL VELVET. She went on to act in many movies such as CLEOPATRA, TAMING OF A SCREW, CAT ON A HOT TIN ROOF, FATHER OF THE BRIDE, A PLACE IN THE SUN, LITTLE WOMEN and more.

Elizabeth Taylor was married eight times. Some of her husbands were Michael Wilding, Eddie Fischer, Richard Burton and John Ford. Elizabeth Taylor became a superstar. She was married to Richard Burton twice. She was with him at least fifteen years. She had four children during her marriages. In later years Elizabeth Taylor married a man who was at least twenty-two years younger than herself.

Elizabeth Taylor has had many surgeries. She drank and smoked for years. She finally went to the Betty Ford Rehabitation Center to try to overcome drinking alcoholic beverages. She lives in the hills of Bel Air in California in a lovely home in the woods. Her gate is locked at the entrance to her long driveway to her home. She has a large swimming pool with a lovely view to the pool and woodlands nearby. Elizabeth's mother lived with her in later years until her mother passed away. Elizabeth was born in 1932 on February 27th. She has traveled around the world.

Richard Burton was from Wales in Great Britain. He grew up in a coal miner's town. He was adopted by the Burtons, which became his last name. Richard Burton began acting in high school plays and then town hall stage plays. He continued with an acting career. He acted in major roles in CLEOPATRA, HAMLET, TAMING OF A SCREW, WHOSE AFRAID OF VIRGINIA WOLF?, THE ROBE, VIPS and many other films. He acted in at least five films with Elizabeth Taylor.

Cary Grant became a super star. He was from England. He began in Vaudeville and performed acrobatic stunts. He became a stunt man in Hollywood as time went by. Then he acted in small roles first. He went on to act in major roles in NORTH BY NORTHWEST, TOUCH OF MINK, CHARADE, BABY, PHILADELPHIA STORY and many more films. Cary Grant eventually became a producer of films. He was married to the millionaire, Barbara Hutton. Cary Grant was married again. He had a child from his third marriage once he divorced Barbara Hutton.

Rex Harrison was from Leister, England. He played major roles such as MY FAIR LADY, DOCTOR DOLITTLE, HAMLET, MAN IN THE DARK and more films. His English accent was interesting to listen to. He was married several times. He traveled in caravan tours across Europe and other places.

John Wayne was a super star. He was in many films. He played major roles as cowboys, soldiers and romantic characters. John Wayne acted in many films produced by John Ford. Many scenes were filmed in Utah in the desert. John Wayne was married to a Mexican woman. He was happily married. However, he was exposed to radiation poisoning in the Utah desert. He died of radiation poisoning when he was working in the radiation zone. He was a victim of a premature death because of radiation when he was acting in cowboy films.

Movie stars know they are public figures. They are in the news and biographies are written about many actors and actresses lives. The private lives of movie stars are easily noticed and they are stopped in public places by fans and other admirers. They are asked to sign their signatures on paper or books, etc. They should be prepared to meet the public.

——— FORTY-FIVE ———

SELF-REALIZATION

Self realization is a significant step in understanding our purpose for existence. We may be confused and ignorant for many years because we haven't looked within to search for the inner truths of our real self.

Self realization occurs when a person looks within to search for God reality. This individual learns to recognize his or her God presence. Once the soul recognizes his or her God presence this soul realizes and identifies with God awareness.

God awareness is a stream of higher consciousness which is expressed from an inner voice within. This inner voice is the higher consciousness coming from the higher self. The higher self enlightens the outer mind.

Gautama Buddha, who lived in India five hundred years before Jesus Christ, searched for inner truth and enlightenment. He developed an eight fold path of enlightenment. He focused on right action, right concentration, right occupation, right morals, right communications, right awareness and right health. Gautama

Buddha learned to live by this eight fold path. Buddha developed self-realization while he meditated under a Bo tree at the edge of a jungle in India.

Jesus Christ was an enlightened soul with self-mastery. Jesus listened to his inner, higher self. He maintained flames of freedom. He lived by the will of God. He set an example for humanity by living the Golden Rule and by brotherhood.

FORTY-SIX

USE YOUR IMAGINATION

Using your imagination is a worthwhile endeavor. You are able to be creative in a variety of ways. A creative person imagines how to write descriptive poetry. Artistic awareness takes imagination. Different styles of painting, pottery making, use of mosaic and geometric designs and free expression are creative ways to express one's imagination.

Imagination is an ongoing experience where individuals feel free to respond to their environment through their five senses. Creative thinking perpetuates remarkable results with the use of colors, words, shapes, designs, textures, scenery, artifacts and inventions.

People who use their imagination change the world with their creations and creative endeavors and unique use of their imagination. Every unique ideas, new style and creative expression adds enrichment to the world. Creative people inspire others to use their imagination.

—— FORTY-SEVEN ——

HOUSEHOLD FIGURINES

Household figurines add beauty and artistic style to a home, an office, churches and other public buildings. Figurines are usually made of glass, porcelain, brass, metal, gold, clay and plastic. They can be arranged on shelves, on pianos, on floors and near gardens, on terraces and balconies, on tables and mantles.

Each figurine is unique and decorative. Figurines are different shapes and colors. Some figurines are more unusual than other figurines. Large, artisan vases with painted designs usually look good in gardens and on terraced patios.

Glass menageries look very intriguing in shelves and window panels. Venetian glass objects are delicate and colorful. There are blown glass objects made in Venice. Wine goblets, vases, jars, bottles, animal and flower figurines are created with Venetian glass. Other glass blowing factories around the world also produce glass figurines.

The story entitled THE GLASS MENAGERIE is a well known story about a girl's fascination of a collection of glass blown figurines which were kept on a special shelf. These figurines were colorful, unique and delicate.

Household figurines add to the décor of your home. You should clean and polish your figurines to keep them shiny and interesting to observe.

——— FORTY-EIGHT ———

TEMPLE CONVENTIONS

The Temple of the People in Halcyon, California in San Luis Obispo County, has a Temple Convention in the first week of August every year. The Temple of the People was established in 1898. The Temple has existed 111 years. Temple Conventions began in 1905.

Each Temple Convention has had a different theme. A message from the Master Hilarion is presented on the first Sunday during the Temple Convention. This Master's message is read to everyone who attends the Sunday meeting.

The Temple Convention begins on the first Saturday night in the Hiawatha Lodge from 7 p.m. until around 9 p.m. A special program of music and drama is presented. Usually a theme is focused on and Social Science talks are presented on Monday or Tuesday at 10 a.m. in The Temple of the People. Anyone who wants to participate may come up to the podium to present a single spaced, typed one page talk about the theme. Through the years many topics have been presented.

During the Temple Conventions there are potlucks in the Hiawatha Lodge and Central Home, There is a garden tour of Halcyon gardens. A children's program is usually presented on the second, Saturday night. A Temple Builders program is presented on the second Sunday morning at 10:30 a.m. in the Temple of the People.

The purpose of Temple Conventions are so people from other places can come from miles away and attend Temple Conventions. It is a time to welcome newcomers and people from around the world.

—— FORTY-NINE ——

SCIENTISTS OF THE WORLD

Scientists have changed our perception of life and the world with their scientific discoveries and scientific methods. The Greeks and Romans developed scientific discoveries about our Universe. They named constellations after Greek and Roman gods and goddesses.

Galileo was an astronomer in Europe over 500 years ago. He invented the first known telescope in Europe. He discovered that the Earth rotates around the Sun in 365 ½ days. He also discovered that the Earth is round. He was the first to discover, during the Renaissance, that the Earth rotates around the Sun. The Catholic pope and his priests rejected Galileo's astronomical discoveries. They forced Galileo to renounce what he discovered. Galileo was imprisoned. Somehow he was able to send his written discoveries outside of Italy to someone who appreciated what he discovered. In time, Galileo's astronomical discoveries were accepted by other scientists and scholars. Galileo is now called the Father of Astronomy.

Carl Sagan is the most famous astronomer of the 20th Century. His discoveries and research have added many new viewpoints to astronomical knowledge. He was involved in the SETI search for ET life.

Stanton Friedman is the most extensively publicized and lecture orientated scientist in UFOlogy. This man has done detailed, meticulous research on secret political, military and intelligence agencies cover-ups of physical, unidentified and technologically superior flying craft. He has accessed hundreds of formerly top secret UFO files from several different nations. Dr. Friedman has interviewed dozens of former military and intelligence agency commanders, officials, pilots, radar operators, astronauts, and other "insiders" to gain the truth about the reality of these craft. Stanton Friedman has compiled an extensive file of credible witnesses proving the Roswell Crash was a fact. Dr. Friedman has compiled over 50 years of his personal, scientific research proving UFOs exist.

Copernicus followed in Galileo's footsteps. He discovered that the Earth is closer to the Sun at certain times of the year. When the Earth is farthest away from the Sun it may be winter in the Northern Hemisphere. It is summer below the equator. Copernicus discovered that the North and South Poles exist and that they effect how the Earth moves around every 24 hours. Copernicus focused on orbits of planets revolving around the Sun.

Sir Isaac Newton, who lived in England approximately three hundred years ago, discovered the law of gravity. He observed an apple fall to the ground. He concluded that gravitational pull caused the apple to fall to the ground. Sir Isaac Newton developed equations about gravity.

Benjamin Franklin discovered electricity by flying a kite which had a metal key. Lightning struck the key and it lit up. Fortunately, Benjamin Franklin wasn't electrocuted. Because of Franklin's discovery of electricity Thomas Edison decided to produce light bulbs of electricity that could be used in electric light bulbs. Today almost everyone on Earth uses electricity.

Nicola Tesla discovered even better ways to conduct electricity. He discovered alternating currents of electricity produces more effective, electrical transmition. Tesla also discovered radar.

Warner Von Braun was the main scientific inventor of the NASA rocket program in the 1940s to 1950s. Astronauts have been able to travel to the Moon. Space modules have been sent to travel around Mars and Saturn. Photos and videos have been taken of the Moon, Venus, Jupiter, Saturn, Neptune, Uranus and Pluto. Photos have been taken of the Earth from outer space modules.

Pierre and Marie Currie were scientists in France in the 20th Century. They discovered radium in their laboratory used to heal diseases today. The Curries' discoveries have benefited the world.

Steve Hawkings has become a well known physicist in the 21st Century who developed the theory about Black Holes which affect our Universe. He has developed the theory that there are parallel universes with parallel dimensions. Black holes exist in the physical universe.

—— FIFTY ——

NEW GENERATIONS BRING CHANGE

Each generation has different attitudes and differences which bring changes. New hair styles, different clothes fashions and slang words accompany each generation. Each decade an up and coming generation makes changes that cause different values and beliefs to exist. Each generation contributes their behavior patterns and values to the world.

During the 1950s crew and butch hair cuts and Elvis Presley hair dos were popular. Girls wore long wavy or curly hairstyles and short straight hair. Girls wore peddle pushers and hoops under long skirts. Harmful, illegal drugs were not heard of at schools in the 1950s. However, marijuana was used by some teenagers and adults. Teenagers and young adults liked to jitterbug on the dance floor. Drag racing was common. Teenagers challenged each other on the drag strip. Teenage gangs were formed.

In the 1960s there was unrest on college campuses. College students complained about the unfair grading by college professors. They also were concerned about political issues and the war in Vietnam. Hair styles continued to change. The hippie generation were called "flower children." They wore unconventional clothes. More and more college students and high school students experimented with harmful drugs. Long hair became popular on males and females. Alternative clothing that was very different from 1950s fashions became popular, as well as foreign clothing styles. In the late 1960s millions of teenagers and adults became very interested in metaphysics, Eastern philosophy and the New Age Movement existed as well as the civil rights movement and environmentalism came into existence.

In the late 1970s unrest on college campuses had greatly decreased after several years of violent revolution by the New Left organizations and leaders. A new generation was concerned about the Watergate scandal. Government politicians were corrupt because they robbed the American treasury causing American tax money to disappear. Americans began to become aware of corruption in politics in the American government. In the late 1970s punk music, fashions, hair and their angry lifestyle became a fad with teenagers and young adults. Meanwhile, millions of youth followed the alternative, yuppie lifestyle that included disco dancing and music, greasers, disco fashions, glamour and hair trimmed short on the top and long on the back. Cocaine was a popular drug of the yuppie society. In that era there was also a fad to bring back the late 1950s youth culture.

The 1980s was a time of transition and reflection. In 1989 the Wall in East Berlin in Germany fell. Germany had transformed and East Berliners were free to go to other places in Germany. The Soviet Union ended and many Communist dictatorships in the Soviet Bloc became democracies. Many clothing fashions were acceptable. The hippy style of living was no longer widespread. The "greening of America" was important. Younger generations were seeking ways to be materially successful and to make more money. Owning attractive homes was important to many people who were seeking a materialistic way of life. Popular hair, fashions, music, movies and culture with teenagers and young adults was called New Wave. Instead of spikes, Mohawks and bizarre punk style hair, New Wave hair was very short and often neat. However, like punk hair it came dyed in all colors of the spectrum. Very bright "day-glow" colors were popular fashions.

In the 1990s during the Clinton Administration America maintained peace and goodwill. Bill Clinton focused on paying the national debts. Gas and oil had increased in price since the last administration. Health needs were addressed. The focus on a better education became more important. Millions of young people took part in the rap and hip-hop fad which focused on a lot of anger, rebellion, violence, drugs and radical sex. This movement was the opposite of the 1960s peace and love movement. Unfortunately, much of this culture was expressed in widespread radio, TV, videos and music. Gang culture and fashions influenced this movement. An alternative was the late 1990s Techno Big Band Movement led by Brian Seltzer. Orchestra music, lyrics, melodies and dances from the 1930s and 1940s were blended with new music technology to create some fun music and ballroom dancing. Many teenagers and young adults were attracted to this style and a large following of participants wore 1940s-style zoot suits and other contemporary fashions.

In the 2000 years, younger generations, as well as older generations, have been concerned about the political and economic issues in the Middle East, especially in Iraq and Afghanistan. The Bush Administration attacked Iraq. Younger generations have been sent to fight in the Middle East after 9-11 in 2001. The war in Afghanistan has been going on for over eight years and the Iraq war over six years. Many Americans wish the wars in the Middle East would end. A big difference in the younger generations of the 1960s and 1970s and the 2000s is that millions in those former generations participated in the anti-war movement and demonstrations. There are far less demonstrations against these new wars and most of the protestors are over fifty years old.

The younger generations in 2000 to 2009 are striving to make ends meet. Many young people must pay rent because they cannot afford to invest in a home. Many young people are looking for suitable employment. They would like to have the same opportunity as previous generations have had to go to college, receive a degree and then obtain worthwhile occupations. Many younger generations are worried about the safety of America. They want to have a bright and prospective future. Many couples are not legally married. Many younger people don't care if they get married. They may have many relationships with the opposite sex, which has been a popular trend since the mid 1960s. Homosexually is also accepted by many men and there are more lesbians. Younger generations are occurring where almost anything is excepted. Many young people follow the fads of any of the last five decades. However, clothing and hair styles that prevail among today's youth are mostly similar to the conservative 50s and early 60s. Today's greasers, beatniks, hippies, mods, yuppies, punks and New Wavers are minorities. However, there is still a big following for rap and hip-hop.

—— FIFTY-ONE ——

OVERCOMING DISEASES

The way to overcome diseases is to avoid being exposed to people who have contagious diseases. We need to maintain a strong, immune system. How can we establish a strong immune system? We need to breathe clean, fresh air. We need to eat fresh, organic fruits and vegetables. Organic grains and raw nuts are good to eat. To exercise regularly is vital to maintain a stronger physical body.

Certain diseases such as different cancers can be avoided by not smoking, drinking excessive alcohol and eating large amounts of red, fatty meat which isn't fresh. Some meats carry disease. Even some polluted fish may carry diseases. It is vital to eat quality, healthy food. Meat and poultry sold in most restaurants and markets are raised on pesticide poison ranges, shot up with dangerous antibiotics and hormones passed on to humans. The hormones used to make cattle, sheep, pigs and poultry fatter to fetch a higher price are passed on to people making them fatter. The drugs injected into these farm animals contain ingredients toxic to human beings. Meat called "lean" with the fat stripped off is still full of dangerous, saturated trans-fats. Small amounts of meat taken over many years add up to great dangers in accumulative toxins and trans fats. By the way, scientists have proven it takes more energy to digest meat than the body receives from it!

Vegetables and fruits purchased in the typical market, café or restaurant are sprayed with deadly pesticides and grown in chemically depleted soil. Organic produce may have four to five times more nutrients than non-organic fruits and vegetables of the same quantity! Also, organic products from health food stores do not contain the very dangerous, genetic engineered GMO of most store and restaurant meals.

Unfortunately, much of the sea life caught these days for food has absorbed the pollution dumped into our oceans passed on to humans. Shell fish are often the most contaminated. Even deadly mercury has been found in thousands of fish.

It is said that many people are addicted to dangerous foods like others are to dangerous drugs. Many fast food manufacturers intentionally put ingredients into their products that are proven addictive. Many of the artificial flavorings and preservatives in most super market and restaurant food contain toxins, that when taken over many years, cause many serious diseases. You can avoid these ailments by buying most of your food at a reputable, organic health food store. Most people can stay healthy with a small portion of their diet from chemical foods. Yet, most of the diet should be non-GMO organic foods for the best resistance to disease! A vegan diet has been proven, in numerous scientific studies in different nations, to be far healthier than a carnivorous or dairy diet. Pasteurization destroys many of the vital nutrients in dairy products. Organic tofu is a substitute for dairy nutrients. Many vegan items contain complete protein.

Overeating and undereating both may cause unnecessary diseases. Our physical bodies need enough of the proper nutrients in order to maintain good health.

It is important to keep your teeth and gums clean everyday. Clean teeth helps us stay healthy. We should take a shower or bath regularly to keep our skin and hair clean and healthy. Cleanliness is Godliness in action.

Live in an environment where the air is clean and fresh. Maintain a harmonious home environment so you can feel at peace. Become one with nature. Keep aware of health concepts and information to awaken you to healthy habits and better ways to maintain good health.

To prevent arthritis and other diseases in the muscles and joints do yoga stretches and exercises. A daily workout of aerobics also strengthens immunity to disease. Avoid a sedentary lifestyle. Thorough university research recommends at least twenty minutes of vigorous physical exercise almost daily. The latest research suggests that to gain health benefits from walking a minimum of three miles at a fast pace is sufficient to stay in shape. Remember that the two leading causes of disease in the last two decades is insufficient exercise and being overweight. Many people have lost that weight by at least twenty minutes of vigorous exercise daily, avoiding fattening foods and eating a vegan diet.

If you come down with a disease you should have it diagnosed by a physician. You may have to take certain medications in order to get well. However, extensive research by many medical studies has proven that nearly all medications have dangerous side effects to be considered. One of the three leading causes of death and disease in America is medications. These results are because of incompatible mixes with other medications and foods, over-doses or toxic chemicals in these drugs. There is a natural, organic cure with no side effects for all major diseases. Most major cities have these professional, natural doctors.

Most diseases can be cured. It just takes time for them to be arrested and overcome. Don't give up in overcoming diseases. Have faith in yourself and be sure to pick a reputable doctor who is not getting money from a pharmaceutical company to prescribe a dangerous drug. If you can find an honest doctor have faith. Continue to eat properly, receive fresh clean air with an abundance of healthy negative ions and exercise properly and regularly. Think in a positive manner because stress and worry damage the immune system! Think in a positive manner about getting well again. Visualize perfect health in daily meditations. Mind over matter can make a huge difference in health. Keep your body slim and active. Get at least ten minutes of sunshine per sunny day because you cannot get vital vitamins like D2 and D3 from any food or beverage. Only the sun can provide these vitamins. Let indirect outdoor sunlight filter into your eyes because sunglasses block vital energy for health. Keep your body alkaline with fresh organic foods, deep breathing negative ions and pure water, with a minimum of toxic chemicals from medicines and meals, to create the strongest immune system. Avoid an over-acidic body caused by legal and illegal drugs, flesh diets, dairy products and excessive food chemical intake, as well as polluted air. If you inhale polluted air, it is a good idea to exhale it in deep breathing exercises using good ions in fresh air.

—— FIFTY-TWO ——

GAINING AND LOSING WEIGHT

It is easy usually to gain weight. If you eat fatty high calorie foods and junk foods you will generally gain weight. You must burn off enough calories to maintain your ideal weight. If you eat balanced meals with a minimum of carbohydrates you may be able to lose weight. However, you also need daily, vigorous exercise for a minimum of twenty minutes.

People, who go on diets to lose weight, usually are expected to eat less food. Their carbohydrates are very restricted. They avoid eating fattening foods and greasy foods. Fried foods are avoided because they have more calories.

There are a variety of diets people use. Some people only eat fruit. Some people eat lean meat with fresh vegetables. Potatoes are limited. Pie, cakes, ice cream, cookies, rich puddings, candy, milkshakes and sodas with sugar are forbidden. High calorie desserts cause people to gain weight. French fries are generally cooked in oil causing them to have more calories than baked potatoes.

Food cooked with grease and food combined with sugar add much more calories to the food. Higher calories must be burned up. Otherwise, they cause a person to gain weight. To lose weight takes discipline and careful planning to eat right in order to lose weight.

Jenny Craig's weight loss program has been tried by many people. She prepares low calorie foods and has them packaged so participants can receive the prepared foods in containers delivered to their homes. The Jenny Craig diet has worked for many people.

The Nutrisystem diet also has been developed. Low calorie foods are packaged and delivered at customers homes. This program has been successful. Nutritional foods are combined in this diet.

A combination of a well balanced low-fat, nutritional diet plus effective exercising will make it easier to lose weight and to keep the unwanted pounds off over a long period of time. However, if you do not get proper daily vigorous exercise you will still gain weight. We are usually healthier when we are able to control our weight because being overweight is a Leading cause of diabetes, heart disease, strokes, weakness and other disabilities.

One of the most effective ways of losing weight is a week, or more of fasting each month until the desired weight is attained. Fasting can be accomplished on juice with all the daily nutrients, such as wheat grass juice, or spiraling, pure fruit or mixed, vegetable juices. Make sure these juices are fresh and organic. You can add organic, protein powder with 100% of your daily protein. This way you stay healthy while fasting.

FIFTY-THREE

LIFE IN ISRAEL

Jerusalem is the capital and major city in Israel. Israel is in the Near East. Jerusalem is where the Star of David Temple was built, which is the largest Jewish synagogue in the world.

There is a wailing wall in Jerusalem where many Jews go to pray and even grieve about their concerns. The climate is generally pleasant in Israel. Jews are domesticated and agriculturally minded. They grow fruit trees and a variety of vegetables.

Many Israelites live in Kibbutz's. A Kibbutz is a commune where families live together. Jews, Arabs and Palestinians live in Israel. There has been a feud between the Israelites and Palestinians over the land. The Israelites took land away from the Palestinians by force. Bickering has continued between the Israelites and the Palestinians over land for many years. The Palestinians have been treated unfairly.

Bethlehem was the birth place of Jesus Christ approximately 2000 years ago. He was born in a nearby cave. A bright object, which appeared to be a star, was seen over the place where Jesus was born. Bethlehem has become a well known place in Israel because Jesus was born there.

Tel Aviv is a seaport city near the Mediterranean Sea in Israel. Tel Aviv is an international city in the Near East. Many tourists travel to Tel Aviv on cruise ships in the Mediterranean Sea. There are many cultural activities as well as museums, art galleries and historic sites to enjoy in Tel Aviv.

There are beautiful valleys throughout Israel. Some other locations are traditional places in Israel such as Bethany, Jaffa, Haifa, Nazareth, Yatta and Hebron. Many Jews live in these places.

Israel is part of the free world in the Near East. It is part of the United Nations. The United States of America supports Israel and protects this country.

——— FIFTY-FOUR ———

LIFE OF MONKEYS, APES AND GORILLAS

Monkeys, apes and gorillas live in jungles in Africa and India. They survive best in trees in jungles. They live in groups. They eat fruit, roots and some jungle vegetation.

Monkeys climb across long branches in jungles. They swing across the branches with their agile tails and arms. They eat bananas, tree fruit such as mangos and berries on the ground. Monkeys are mammals. When they are born they depend on milk from their mothers when they are babies. They eventually learn to eat tree fruit, roots and berries, etc.

Grooming is an important procedure which monkeys perform on each other. Mother monkeys pull lice and sucking insects out of baby monkeys. This regular cleansing helps to keep their young ones alive. Mother monkeys are very protective of their young. Baby monkeys cling to their mothers until they are winned. Baby monkeys learn to move in trees and on the ground with their parents.

Monkeys continue to swing around into many trees. They have enemies such as tigers, leopards, panthers and human hunters who are predators. Monkeys must be on the lookout for their predators. They are capable of rushing away across the branches to escape from their enemies who attempt to attack them during daytime and nighttime.

Monkeys are primates and live in groups. They have a dominate male who leads the group. They usually stay close together. Young monkeys like to play with one another. Monkeys can be identified by their individual habits and behavior. They tend to be emotional. They find food in the jungles.

Apes and gorillas are much larger than monkeys. Apes and gorillas live in groups. They also move in trees and thick bushes. They eat fruit, some vegetation and roots. Female apes and gorillas look after their young primates. Male apes and gorillas protect their females and young apes and gorillas from dangers. They rush away from human hunters if they sense danger. The dominant, male leader appears quite fierce to scare away anyone who invades their territory.

Baboons, monkeys, gorillas and apes have been captured to be put in zoos. They do not like to be captured. They need a comfortable environment at zoos. They need water as well as fruit and vegetables to eat. Trees and branches should be in large cages so they can move around readily.

Jane Goodell went to Mt. Kilimanjaro in Africa to study gorillas who lived in a dense jungle region there. She studied their habits and behavior. She found out how they survived and related to each other. Gorillas respond to affection. They have one mate as a rule. They live in groups and they mate regularly.

FIFTY-FIVE

JUNGLE ADVENTURES

Jungles are dense, verdant growth where many jungle animals and insects live. Wild animals that live in jungles are tigers, leopards, panthers, wild boars, monkeys, apes, gorillas, anteaters, parrots, parakeets, cockatoos, orangutans, chimpanzees, sloths and lions. Zebras and gazelles live in savannahs close to jungles. Jungles are usually hot and humid. There are a variety of jungle snakes.

Jungle animals must protect themselves from predators. They must be on the lookout all the time from being attacked and eaten. The weakest creatures and unobservant animals usually are the first to get caught and eaten. The most fit creatures usually live the longest because they are stronger and healthier.

Warren and Alexandria Foster, a young couple from New Jersey, decided to travel to the Congo in Central Africa. They packed their backpacks with appropriate clothing and supplies to use in the Congo jungle.

They boarded a public plane to Africa from the John F. Kennedy Airport in New York City, America.

When the public plane landed near the Congo, Warren and Alexandria Foster walked off the airplane into the African airport. It was very warm outside. Ceiling fans were on indoors to cool the arrival and departure sitting rooms. Warren and Alexandria collected their backpacks at the arrivals section.

Warren and Alexandria rented a jeep. They put their backpacks in the jeep. Their backpacks included nets, bedding, a tent for two people, machetes, ropes and comfortable clothing to wear in the jungle. They had an extra pair of walking boots to wear in the jungle. Warren drove the jeep with Alexandria at his side.

The Congo was miles down the road. It took several hours to arrive in the jungle. Warren parked the jeep at the edge of the jungle. Warren and Alexandria unpacked the jeep. They each carried a backpack on their backs. They took out machetes to carve their way through the dense jungle. They cut entangled limbs and thick twigs. Thick grass and sword ferns were growing everywhere close to jungle trees.

Warren and Alexandria began cutting thick foliage away so they could walk through the dense jungle. They heard the sound of birds and jungle animals as they continued their walk into the jungle. They saw snakes slithering in jungle trees. Some of the snakes were hanging down toward the jungle floor.

Alexandria saw a long, green snake crawling very close to where she was walking. She cut twigs and twines away to move on. The snake fell down close to her. Alexandria backed away from the snake. She wasn't sure if it was poisonous. Warren took his machete and cut the snake in half so it wouldn't attack Alexandria or himself.

Warren and Alexandria continued walking further into the jungle. They saw monkeys crawling and swinging up in the taller trees. Some monkeys were chattering and eating jungle fruit in the trees. They stared at Warren and Alexandria. Alexandria and Warren continued forging their way ahead. They saw a wild boar in the distance. It was moving about in the entwined foliage. The wild boar made a grunting sound. It ran in the opposite direction to get away from Warren and Alexandria.

The Fosters finally came to the end of the jungle. They were tired after walking this far. They decided to clear a space so they could pitch their tent. They hammered stakes into the jungle floor. Warren pulled the tent up and tied ropes around the stakes in the ground. Once the tent was up and secured Alexandria unrolled the bedding inside the tent. She brought the backpacks inside the ten foot tent. She removed twine and twigs from the floor of the tent. The tent had an opening on one side.

Warren and Alexandria were tired from walking and cutting entangled limbs and twigs. They laid down on their bedding to rest. It was hot and humid in the jungle. Warren and Alexandria covered themselves with nets to keep mosquitoes and other biting insects from stinging them.

While they rested, Warren and Alexandria used hand fans to cool off their faces. They could hear wild animals and jungle birds around them. They hoped no intruders would invade their tent. They rested for several hours. Then they heard a very loud sound that woke them up. They were worried what was happening outside the tent.

It was beginning to get dark. Then it started to rain. The rain continued to drop to the jungle floor. The trees and jungle foliage were dripping with rain. The rain helped to cool the jungle.

Warren and Alexandria waited for the rain to stop while they remained in their tent. The loud sound had stopped. The Fosters were hungry. Alexandria opened a can of spaghetti for Warren and her to eat. She unpacked some bananas and mangos. She cut the mangos into pieces. She pealed some bananas. She put the fruit on two plates.

Alexandria and Warren shared the can of cold spaghetti. They ate the fruit. Then they sipped some bottled water. This was the extent of their meal. It was getting darker. So, Warren and Alexandria decided to stay in their tent until the next morning when the sun came out again. They spoke to each other about their plans for the next day. Then they prepared their clothes which they would wear the next day. Once again, they rested to restore themselves for the next day.

Late at night Warren and Alexandria woke up because they heard something scratching at their tent. They became worried about this scratching. They had a netted window with a covering over the window. Warren had zipped up the door much earlier before Alexandria and he had laid down to rest. Warren looked out the netted window. He saw a large, black panther staring at him. It continued to claw at the tent.

Warren decided to take a limb he had kept in the tent. He used the limb as a weapon to scare the panther away. He hit the limb against the side of the tent where the panther was clawing. He yelled at the panther to go away as he continued to hit the side of the tent. Fortunately the tent remained standing. The black panther finally retreated from the tent and ran away. Warren and Alexandria were relieved. They continued to rest until the sun came up the next morning.

The next morning Warren and Alexandria changed into different clothes. They ate sliced fruit. They opened a can of spam. Alexandria cut the spam into slices for them to eat. They drank some bottled water. After breakfast they took the tent down and folded it up. They repacked their backpacks and cleaned up the area where they had camped. It was time to continue their trek through the jungle. They wore insect repellant on their faces, arms and legs. They wore their boots. Warren and Alexandria carried their backpacks on their backs. They continued walking through the jungle. They used their machetes to cut away more foliage. The sun was beaming through the dense jungle.

Suddenly, a tiger appeared nearby and glared at Warren and Alexandria with piercing eyes. It stood there within 16 feet from where Warren and Alexandria were cutting the foliage away. Warren didn't have a gun on him. He pointed his machete knife toward the orange and black spotted tiger to ward it away. The tiger backed off and walked away. Warren and Alexandria continued cutting foliage as they trekked through the dense jungle.

Some unusual, tropical birds which were multi-colored with bright red, yellow, green and white were chirping in different jungle trees. Alexandria took some photographs of these rare birds. The sun beamed through the trees. It became warm and insects were flying around. They landed on jungle plants. Fortunately, Warren and Alexandria were protected by nets over their faces which were held down by jungle hats. Their arms and legs were covered with more insect repellent to keep insects from biting them.

After trekking for another hour or so, Warren and Alexandria came to an African tribal village of thatched twine huts which had no windows or modern conveniences. African natives wore very little clothing. Native men wore a twine strip over their private parts. Native women wore a twine cloth over their lower, private parts. Their breasts were exposed and very visible. The African tribe were dark skinned with dark brown eyes and kinky, black hair. They wore a colored band around their hair.

Warren and Alexandria noticed around thirty-five African men and women in this tribal village. Warren and Alexandria approached the tribal villagers. They began to speak to them. However, the natives didn't speak any English. Warren finally used sign language to communicate with the tribe's people.

A tribesman called Ogo responded with sign language when Warren asked who these tribes people were. Warren pointed to Alexandria and then himself and said "Warren" for himself and "Alexandria" for his wife. Ogo pointed to himself and said, "Ogo." Warren pointed to several other tribesmen standing nearby. Ogo replied, as he pointed to each tribesman. Ogo pointed to the first man near him. He said, "Emo." Then he pointed to the second tribesman. He said, "Umu." He pointed to another tribesman. He said, "Gio." Warren and Alexandria smiled at the tribes people they had just met. The tribes people finally repeated "Warren" and "Alexandria."

Ogo showed Warren and Alexandria around the small village. Ogo brought out some bananas and other jungle fruit for Warren and Alexandria to eat. They sat on the ground with the tribes people and ate the tropical fruit. Warren and Alexandria were glad these African people were friendly. They noticed they had primitive spears.

Warren and Alexandria were welcome to stay in the village overnight. Ogo showed Warren and Alexandria an empty village hut. They put their backpacks into this thatched hut. Then Ogo took Warren and Alexandria to a running stream. They walked into the cool stream. They decided to swim in a deeper part of the stream to cool off and to wash themselves. They splashed around in the moving stream. Tribes people walked into the stream to swim and to enjoy the cool water. They decided to swim in a deeper part of the stream to cool off and to wash themselves. They splashed around in the moving water. Everyone relaxed in the stream.

After swimming in the four foot pool, Warren and Alexandria came out of the water within a half hour. The tribe people eventually came out of the water. Ogo decided to climb a tall tree nearby to hunt for a beehive. He found a beehive high up in a tall tree. He saw many bees buzzing around the hive. Some bees stung Ogo. He managed to knock the beehive out of the tree with a stick. The hive landed on the ground below the tree. Some bees were still hovering inside the hive.

Ogo took a stick and cracked open the beehive. Honey nectar was stored in wax containers. Ogo broke the wax sections so everyone could enjoy eating some honey. This honey nectar was a real treat for these African natives. Warren and Alexandria enjoyed tasting the honey nectar. They stayed overnight in the primitive, thatched hut that night.

Before going to bed Ogo invited Warren and Alexandria to sit outside in a circle to hear tribal music. Tribes people chanted different tribal songs. They danced in a group. Their body movements were unique. Drums were tapped rhythmically while tribal men and women danced their tribal movements.

The Moon came out and lit the sky and jungle. The air had cooled off in the evening after the Sun had disappeared over the horizon. After chanting and dancing it was time for everyone to go to bed. Warren and Alexandria went to the hut they were to stay in. They laid out their bedding and laid down to rest. They felt safer staying in this African village near the friendly African people.

The next morning Warren and Alexandria woke up when it was light outside. They got up and went outside after dressing in their jungle clothes. Ogo, Emo, Umu and Gio as well as other tribesmen greeted them. Ogo offered Warren and Alexandria cooked monkey meat for breakfast. So, Alexandria and Warren sampled the monkey meat. It tasted alright. Ogo and other tribesmen had speared several monkeys high in the jungle trees to use for village meals. Warren and Alexandria spent three more days in this village learning about this tribe.

Warren and Alexandria thanked the African tribes people using sign language. They packed their belongings. It was time to move on. The Fosters shook hands with the tribal villagers as a token of farewell. They left the small village and continued their journey into the jungle. They remembered to put insect repellant on their skin first.

The Fosters saw more wild, jungle animals as they walked in the jungle, such as anteaters, sloths and some orangutans and apes. These jungle creatures were fascinating to observe. They saw jungle spiders in their webs and red, large, jungle ants carrying jungle leaves along the jungle floor. The Fosters learned how they survived in the jungle.

Warren and Alexandria finally went back to their jeep after many hours of trekking in the jungle. They drove back to the airport. They boarded a passenger plane after spending a week in the Congo in Africa. They had enjoyed their jungle adventures.

—— FIFTY-SIX ——

FACTS ABOUT AMERICA

The United States of America is made up of 50 states and American Commonwealths and territories. The national bird is the Bald Eagle. The national flower is the rose. The northern most point in the U.S.A. is Point Barrow in Alaska. Cape Wrangel in Alaska is the westernmost point in the U.S.A. Each year it rains about 460 inches in the wettest place in the world at Mt. Waileale, Kauai in Hawaii. Denali is the highest mountain in North America. It is 20,320 feet. Ka Lae in Hawaii is the southernmost point in the U.S.A. The Mississippi River is 2,348 miles long. It is the longest river in North America. Lake Superior, bordering Canada and the United States is the largest freshwater lake in the world. The St. Lawrence Seaway is the longest canal in the world. It is about 450 miles long and borders Canada and the United States. The easternmost point in the U.S.A. is West Ouoddy Head, Maine. Death Valley is the lowest spot in the nation at 282 feet below sea level in California.

In ALABAMA, the Heart of Dixie, people lived in Russell Cave for 8,000 years from 6,500 B.C. to 1500 A.D. We know because they left bones and tools behind. Alabama's state bird is the Yellow-shafted flicker and is called the Yellow Hammer. George Washington Carver (1864-1943) was an agricultural scientist at Tuskegee University, who developed hundreds of uses for peanuts and sweet potatoes in the early 1900s. The state tree is the southern pine. Alabama is famous for its pine forests. The trees are made into paper products, the state's biggest industry.

Alabama's state flower is the camellia. The state insect is the monarch butterfly which flies to Mexico for the winter. The Mississippian mound builders built temple mounds for ceremonies. One in Moundville is still standing after 800 years. Alabama has many miles of beautiful beaches on the Gulf of Mexico.

In ALASKA the Aurora Borealis is the northern lights display that brightens the 24-hour winter nights. In the summer Alaska is the land of the midnight sun. Alaska is about one-fifth as large as the United States. Juneau is the only state capital that cannot be reached by road. The state flower is the Forget-me-nots. Kodiak Island is home to the largest known bears on Earth. Humpback whales are often seen in summer off Alaska's coast, where cold arctic waters provide plenty of rich plankton to eat.

In ARIZONA the Grand Canyon is a scenic 277 mile long gorge that is one mile deep in some places. Canyon de Chilly was home to prehistoric Pueblo Indians. The state flower is the saguaro cactus, the largest cactus in the U.S.A. It blooms in the Sonoran Desert. Geronimo (1829-1909) was a legendary Apache leader. In 1886 his tribe was one of the last to surrender to U.S. troops in Skeleton Canyon. The Tucson area is called the Astronomy Capital of the world because of the good star viewing away from the city lights. Hoover Dam regulates the flow of the Colorado River. Its huge generators use the energy of the moving water to make electricity.

In Arkansas, the land of opportunity and the 15th state, Blanchard Spring Caverns elevators take visitors to caves like the Cathedral Room, a cave as long as four football fields. The state instrument is a fiddle, which is another name for a violin that plays bluegrass music. The state gem is a diamond. The state flower is the apple blossom. The state bird is the mocking bird.

In CALIFORNIA, the Golden State and 31st state, Cesar Chavez was a Mexican-American labor leader who peacefully organized migrant grape pickers and farm workers in the 1960s. The state tree is the California redwood which are the tallest trees in the world. Some are 368 feet tall. Yosemite National Park has some of the highest waterfalls and deepest valleys in the U.S.A. Giant sequoia trees can be 100 feet around and live over

2,000 years. The Golden Gate Bridge spans the entrance to San Francisco Bay. La Brea Tar Pits in Los Angeles have rich deposits of Ice Age fossils. The state flower is the Golden Poppy. The state bird is the California valley quail. It was 134 degrees F in Death Valley in 1913, the highest temperature ever recorded in the U.S.A. Death Valley is also the lowest point of dry land in the U.S.A.

In COLORADO, the Centennial State and the 38th state, gold and silver are mined in the Rocky Mountains. In 1894, the larges, silver nugget (1,840 pounds) in North America was unearthed in Aspen. Ancient Anasazi cliff dwellings exist. Large dinosaur fossil deposits are found in Colorado. Denver, the mile high city, is 5,280 feet above sea level. The cry of the 1858 gold rush was in "Pike Peak or Bust." The state flower is the Rocky Mountain columbine. The Colorado Mountains have some of the best skiing in the world. The state tree is the Blue Spruce. The state bird is the lark bunting which nests in the dry sagebrush plains and prairies of Colorado. The Continental Divide stretches the length of the Colorado Rockies. Water rushes off east to the Atlantic Ocean and west to the Pacific Ocean.

In CONNECTICUT, the Constitution State, the Mountain Laurel adorns woodlands and roadsides. Noah Webster (1758-1843) was a journalist and teacher who wrote the first American dictionary and he was from Connecticut. The state bird is the robin. Eli Whitney became the father of mass production in Connecticut when he made muskets with uniform, interchangeable parts in the early 1800s. The state tree is the white oak. Connecticut is known as the Constitution State.

In DELAWARE, the First State in 1638, near the south of the Delaware River, Swedish and Finnish settlers built the first big cabins in North America. The state flower is the peach blossom. Nylon was invented in 1938 in Wilmington in Delaware, making Delaware a leader in the chemical industry. Most of this state was once covered by the ocean. Many extinct fossilized sea creatures have been found here. The state bird is the Blue hen chicken. The northernmost cypress swamp in the U.S.A. is an ancient bald-cypress and cedar forest. The state tree is the American holly that has separate male and female trees.

In FLORIDA, the Sunshine State, 80% of the nation's oranges and grapefruits are grown. The state flower is the orange blossom. The state bird is the mocking bird. The oldest European settlement in North America was founded at St. Augustine in 1565. The space shuttle was launched in Cape Canaveral. Pensacola Naval Air Station is home to the Blue Angels, the Navy's famous, aerial flight, acrobatic team. Florida waters have more kinds of fish than any other place in the world. Wild flamingos are now extinct in Florida. The Florida Keys, which is a 150 mile chain of small islands, is connected by a highway. Sunken treasures have been found in Key West. Near Orlando is Epcot Center and Walt Disney

World. Florida has more "champions" or largest living tree specimens than any other state. The Gulf Stream provides the warmest ocean temperatures in the continental United States and South Florida and the Keys have the warmest winters. Florida has hundreds of miles of beautiful, sandy beaches bordered by green vegetation. Miami is one of the most popular, beach resorts in the nation. The Everglades is a spectacular zone of dense vegetation and water located inland, and home to many interesting wildlife species. Florida offers many lakes, forests and streams. An interesting, geographical fact is that there are no hills or mountains. Florida is a flat state bordered by sea or ocean on three sides.

In GEORGIA, the Empire State of the South, the state flower is the Cherokee rose. The honeybee is the state insect. In 1947, Jackie Robinson, (1919 to 1972) born in Cairo, Georgia, became the first, black baseball player in the 20th Century to play in the major leagues. American alligators live in freshwater wetlands. The state tree is the live oak. These strong, majestic trees often shade old, southern plantations. Peach County grows many varieties of peaches. Georgia grows more pecans and peanuts (goobers) than any other state. The state bird is the Brown thrasher. Okefenokee Swamp is the largest freshwater swamp in the U.S.A. Georgia is the fourth state.

HAWAII, the Aloha State, is the 50th state in America. The Hawaiian Islands were formed by volcanoes. Some are still active. There are 8 major islands in Hawaii and several other small islands. Lanai once had the largest pineapple plantation in the world. However, today there is diversified agriculture. Lanai remains a tropical paradise because hotels, restaurants, houses and other buildings are not allowed on any beach. The island has the longest and widest beach in the state. A dense, pine forest is located in the interior. Another beach at Manele has been rated the best in Hawaii. The most popular and famous beach in Hawaii is Waikiki, on the island of Oahu. Kauai is the Garden Island because of its beautiful, lush, tropical vegetation. The Big Island of Hawaii is famous for its snowcapped volcanoes high above hot and humid jungles. Niiahau Island is unique because only Hawaiians are allowed to visit and live on this island that has retained Hawaiian culture. Maui has been rated "the best island in the world," over ten times, by Travel and Leisure Magazine and Conde' Nest travel magazine. At sea level there is a warm, tropical climate every month of the year, a continuous spring climate on the slopes of Haleakala and a constant winter climate at an elevation of ten thousand feet. Maui offers tropical rainforests, a desert, farmlands, meadows, savannahs, mountains and palm lined beaches on one island. Hawaii's state bird is the Nene, an island goose that is now rare. Queen Liliuokalani (1838-1917) was the last of Hawaii's royalty to live in the only palace in the U.S.A. Surfing, the oldest sport in the U.S.A., started in Hawaii long before Columbus sailed. The state tree is the kukui tree.

IDAHO is the Gem state and the 43rd in the nation and where potatoes are grown in the fertile Snake River Valley more than in any other place in the U.S.A. Woodland caribou live in coniferous forests near Canada in northern Idaho. Sacagawea, born in Idaho, was a teenage Shoshone who helped guide the Lewis and Clark Expedition from North Dakota to the Pacific Ocean. She carried her baby with her. The Salmon River was named "The River of No Return" for the ferocious rapids. At Sun Valley ski resort, the world's first ski lift began operations in 1935. The state tree is the Western White Pine. The Monarch butterfly is the state insect. The state flower is the Syringa. The Crystal Ice Cave displays formations of ice and stone. The state bird is the mountain bluebird.

ILLINOIS, land of Abraham Lincoln, is the 21st state. Abraham Lincoln (1809 to 1865) was an honest Illinois lawyer, before becoming our 16th President. O'hare Airport is the world's busiest; a plane lands or takes off every 30 seconds. There are more than 30 covered bridges in Parke County. The "El", an elevated train that circles Chicago's downtown "Loop", started running in November, 1897 in Illinois. The state flower is the Violet. The state tree is the White Oak which grows to be over 100 feet tall. The state bird is the Red Cardinal. In 1893, the original Ferris Wheel was built for the World's Columbian Exposition. 2,160 people could ride at one time. Monk's Mound, built by ancient Mississippian people, is the largest Indian mound in North America. Its base is bigger than the Great Pyramid of Egypt.

INDIANA is the Hossier State and the 19th in the nation. Indiana's northeast corner has great steel mills and huge, oil refineries. In 1875, Indiana was the first place in the U.S. to teach girls and boys in the same classroom. The town of Santa Claus has the only U.S. post office named Santa Claus (ZIP code 47579). One of the largest caverns in the U.S.A., Wyandotte has 5 levels and 35 miles of underground passages. The state tree is the Tuliptree. The state flower is the Peony. Indiana's state bird is the Cardinal, which are often seen in pairs.

IOWA is the Hawkeye State. The state flower is a wild rose. The red delicious apple came from shoots of a big lightning-struck tree in the 1800s. Iowas is mostly rich farmland, leading the nation in raising hogs and growing corn. The Missouri and Mississippi rivers are major waterfowl migration routes for thousands of birds in spring and fall. The Iowa Pleistocene snail has lived in coal, moist ground for over 300,000 years. The state insect is the goldfinch. They circle over the fields filling the air with music.

KANSAS is a sunflower state and is the 29th in the nation. Kansas leads the nation in wheat production, making it the "Bread-basket of the world. People built sod houses. Black-capped vireas once thrived on brushy slopes. They no longer breed in Kansas. Amelia Earhart, from Atchison, was the first woman to fly solo across the Atlantic Ocean. Kansas now leads the world in aircraft production. The state tree is the Cottonwood. Trees line the rivers throughout Kansas. The state insect is the honeybee. Thousands of longhorn cattle were driven from Texas to Kansas railroad stations. The state bird is the Meadowlark that hide their nests in prairie grasses where millions of buffalo once roamed. The state flower is the sunflower.

KENTUCKY, the 15th state, is the Bluegrass State. Nutritious bluegrass near Lexington make it the "Thoroughbred Capital of the world." The Mammoth Cave System has 340 miles of underground passages. Over 200 animal species are found here. Daniel Boone (1734 to 1820) led the first white settlers through the dangerous Cumberland Gap into Kentucky in 1775. The state flower is the goldenrod. Since 1875 the Kentucky Derby, a world famous horse race, has been held every May at Churchill Down. The state flower is the tulip-poplar.

LOUISIANA is the Pelican State. It is the 18th state. The state flower is the Magnolia blossom. The state tree is the bald cypress. Thousands of egrets, herons and other birds flock to Avery Island and the swampy woods for safety. The world's largest indoor arena, the Louisiana Superdome in New Orleans, has 95,427 seats. Louisiana crayfish are used in famous Cajun and Creole recipes. Mardi Gras is a holiday celebrated with parades, parties, feasts and costume balls. Everyone wears a mask. The birthplace of jazz was in New Orleans. Louis Satchmo Armstrong (1900 to 1971) was world renowned for his trumpet sounds.

MAINE is the Pine Tree State. It is the 23rd state. Maine's Atlantic coast is rocky and jagged. Lakes and coastlines are ideal for sailing. Millions of pounds of tasty Maine lobsters are sold annually around the world. Portland Head Light is one of Maine's 62 lighthouses. West Quaddy Head is the most easterly point of land in the U.S.A. The state bird is the Chickadee. The state flower is the White Pinecone and tassel. Maine has over 2,500 lakes and 5,000 rivers or streams. The state animal is the Moose and symbolizes Maine's wildlife areas.

MARYLAND is the Old Line State. It is the 7th state. The Chesapeake Bay is 200 miles long and 440 miles wide. The state bird is the Baltimore oriole and the state insect is the Baltimore chekerspot butterfly, named after Lord Baltimore whose family crest was orange and black. Harriet Tubman (1820 to 1913) was born a slave near Cambridge; but escaped in 1849. She led over 300 slaves north to freedom following the North Star. Backbone Mountain is 3,360 feet. The state tree is the White Oak and the state flower is the Black Eyes Susan. The Wye oak tree at Wye Mills is the largest white oak in the U.S.A. It is 400 years old and is 107 feet tall and 34 ½ feet around at its base. Legend has it that the wild ponies of Assateague Island are descendants of horses from a Spanish galleon wrecked in the 1500s. The Mason Dixon Line is the state line between Maryland and Pennsylvania, surveyed by Mason and Dixon. It became the division between slave and free states before the Civil War. Mile markers still exist.

MASSACHUSETTS is the Bay State and it is the 6th state. In 1636 Harvard, the first college in North America was founded in Cambridge. Massachusetts grows half the nation's tangy cranberries. On April 18, 1775, silversmith Paul Revere rode through Lexington warning "The British are coming." Each year millions of tourists visit Nantucket, Cape Cod and Martha's Vineyard. America's oldest (1897) annual long-distance race is the Boston Marathon. The state flower is the Mayflower. Volleyball, an Olympic sport, was invented in Holyoke in 1895. The Mayflower landed at Plymouth Rock in 1620. Half the colony died the first year. Squanto and other natives taught the remaining Pilgrims how to hunt and grow foods to survive. At the harvest, they celebrated peace and sharing---the first Thanksgiving. The state tree is the American elm. The state bird is the Black-capped Chickadee. In 1891, peach baskets were hung 10 feet high on gym balcony railings. Basketball, the world's most popular indoor sport, was born.

MICHIGAN is the Wolverine State and the 26th. Isle Royale is a wilderness home to moose and wolves.

The upper and lower peninsulas are connected by the 5 mile long, Mackinac Bridge. Kirkland's warbler nests only in young jack pines. 4 of the 5 Great Lakes border Michigan, giving it 3,288 miles of shoreline, second only to Alaska. Battle Creek produces more breakfast cereal than anywhere else in the world. It is the "Cereal Bowl of America." The state bird is the robin. Henry Ford invented his first gas-powered automobile in 1896. Michigan is the number one producer of U.S. cars and trucks. The state tree is the White Pine.

MINNESOTA is the Gopher State and the 32nd in the nation. Lake Superior is the largest freshwater lake in the world. Fishing, biking, snow skiing and non-motor boating are popular in Boundary Waters Canoe Area. No cars or hotels are allowed in this wilderness. The state flower is the pink and white Lady's Slipper and is a rare beauty in shady spots. Minnesota is sometimes called "The Land of 1,000 Lakes." The state bird is the Common Loon that dives deep for fish and has an unforgettable, laugh-like call.

MISSISSIPPI, the Magnolia State, is the 20th state. The Natchez Trace Parkway was first established by the Natchez Indians, who formed and made beautiful pottery and fabrics. Later, the trail was heavily used by early flatboat man returning home. It became a national parkway in 1938. Biloxi processes 60 million pounds of shrimp every year. The most important inland waterway in the U.S.A. is the Mississippi River. Riverboats still tour up and down the river. Delta blues music became popular in the 1890s. The state tree is the Magnolia. The gopher tortoise feeds on many grasses and plants in mature pine woodlands.

MISSOURI is the Show Me State and is the 24th state. Pony Express riders relayed the mail, station to station, from St. Joseph to California. They could cover about 2,000 miles in about 10 days of hard riding. Samuel Clemens (1835 to 1910), who grew up in Hannibal, took his pen name Mark Twain, from the depth of water riverboats needed to stay afloat. St. Louis is known as the "Gateway to the West." Ice cream cones originated at the St. Louis World's Fair in 1904. The Missouri bladder pod is found in only 9 places with all of them in Missouri. The state bird is the Bluebird.

MONTANA, the Treasure State, is the 41st in the nation. The Lewis and Clark expedition traveled the great Montana rivers. Many Indians saw their first black man, York, who was on the journey. Almost every Montana town still has an "Old West" rodeo. Montana is home to the grizzly bears and over 50 glaciers. Yellowstone Park is spectacular with high geysers.

NEBRASKA is the Corn Husker State and the 37th in the nation. J. Sterling Morton planted trees in Nebraska for the first Arbor Day, April 10, 1872. Now, Earth Day is celebrated on April 22nd. Corn husking contests were once popular in Nebraska. The state bird is the Meadowlark. Bays Town is a community for homeless kids started December 1917. The Union Pacific Railroad began laying track west from Omaha in 1865. Almost all of Nebraska is farmland. The state flower is the Goldenrod and the state tree is the Cottonwood. The pallid sturgeon ascended from fish living when dinosaurs roamed the Earth.

NEVADA is the Silver State and it is the 36th state. The desert tortoise can survive on little water in the nation's driest state. The Comstock Lode in Virginia City was a gold and silver mining center in 1859 to 1868. Nevada has two state trees which are the single leaf pinon pine and the bristlecone pines. Many ghost towns were once thriving, gold towns. The state flower is the sagebrush. The state bird is the Mountain Bluebird. The energy of the Colorado River is harnessed at Hoover Dam. Las Vegas is the nation's leading entertainment resort and one of the most popular tourist destinations in America.

NEW HAMPSHIRE is the Granite State and it is the 9th in the nation. Old Man of the Mountains is a great stone face on Profile Mountain. The oldest and longest covered buildings still in use in the U.S.A. are in New Hampshire. The first cog railway in the U.S.A. was built in 1869 and still pushes the train into Mt. Washington. Christina McAuliffe (1948-1986), a courageous New Hampshire teacher, was the first private citizen in space. The Christina McAuliffe Planetarium is in Concord. The state tree is the white birch and is also known as the canoe birch. The state bird is the purple finch.

NEW JERSEY is the Garden State and it is the 3rd state. The state tree is the Red Oak Bark which is rich in tanning, used for tanning leather. The state dinosaur, Hadrosaur, was the first dinosaur skeleton discovered in North America was found near Haddonfield in 1858. New Jersey is a leader in producing chemicals. Many people vacation on the white sandy beaches of the Jersey shore. The Raseate tern needs isolated beaches for concealed nests. The Pine Barrens is a wilderness of bogs, salt marshes and swamps. Atlantic City is famous for its wooden boardwalk and saltwater taffy. The Sandy Hook Lighthouse has been guiding ships into port since 1763. The Garden State is famous for its Jersey tomatoes. Trenton is the capital city.

NEW MEXICO is the land of enchantment and it is the 47th state. The state tree is the Prison Tree. New Mexico grows the most chilies in the U.S.A. In 1950, a bear cub was rescued from a forest fire. He became Smokey the Bear. The state bird is the Roadrunner. At dusk tens of thousands of bats emerge from limestone caverns in 24 miles of passages to feast on millions of bugs. There are many caves. The Big Room is the largest natural cave in the world. Hot air balloons from all over the world come to Albuquerque in mid-October. Gallup hosts the intertribal Indian Ceremonial every August. New Mexico's ridge nose rattlesnakes hide out in remote pine and oak woodlands. The sand dunes are so white they glisten like snow fields. Shiprock, or Tse Bit'a'I is a rock formation sacred to the Navajo.

NEW YORK is the Empire State and it is the 11th state. The sugar maple is the source of maple syrup and candy, as well as blazing, autumn colors. Lake Placid was the sight of the 1932 and the 1980 Winter Olympics. The American hart's tongue fern grows in the cool, moist soil of the limestone sinkholes. Mary Jemison was a white child captured by the Seneca Tribe in 1755. The Statue of Liberty was a gift from France in 1884. It stands in New York Harbor. Cooperstown is home to the National Baseball Hall of Fame. Coney Island is a beach resort known for its boardwalk and hot dogs. The United Nations Headquarters are in New York City. From 1892 to 1954 over 12 million immigrants passed through Ellis Island Center. Radio City Theater was open in 1932 in downtown New York City and it seats 5,883 people. The state flower is the Rose. The state bird is the Bluebird.

NORTH CAROLINA is the Tar Heel State and the 12th in the nation. In 1903, the Wright Brothers flew the first plane near Kitty Hawk. "The Lost Colony," Roanoke Island was colonized by the English in 1587. A supply ship returned 3 years later, but the colony had disappeared. The outer banks are long sandbars that lie offshore. They are the site of many shipwrecks. The lighthouse at Cape Hatteras is the tallest brick lighthouse in the U.S.A. North Carolina leads the U.S.A. in textile production. Red wolves hide their dens in swamps. The Venus flytrap grows only in the pinelands and savannahs of North and South Carolina. At Grandfather Mountain, there is a mile high, swinging bridge. The Piedmont region is famous for fine wooden furniture. The state bird is the Cardinal. The state flower is the Flowering Dogwood. The state tree is the Pine.

NORTH DAKOTA is the Flickertail State and is the 39th state. Wheat for pasta grows in the prairies. The Eskimo curlew, now rare, was common in the 1800s. Some of the most desolate but scenic land in the world is in the Badlands. Theodore Roosevelt, nature enthusiast and our 26th President, reached here. The state flower is the wild prairie rose. The Red River Valley has some of the most fertile farmland in the world. The International Peace Garden is a symbol of friendship. Sunflowers grow all over the state. The state tree is the American Elon. The state bird is the Meadowlark. The prairie dogs of North Dakota flick their tails in warning.

OHIO is the Buckeye State and the 17th in the nation. John Chapman (Johnny Appleseed) planted hundreds of acres of apple orchards in Ohio. Raw materials imported on Ohio's rail, water and truck routes are manufactured into products and exported on the same routes. The Pro Football Hall of Fame is in Canton. Seven U.S. presidents were born in Ohio. They were

Grant, Hays, Garfield, Harrison, McKinley, Taft and Harding. The Ohio River is navigable all year long. It empties into the Mississippi River. An Ohio architect, Maya Ying Lin, designed the Vietnam Memorial in Washington D.C. The state flower is the Scarlet Carnation. About 2000 years ago, Indian mound builders came to the Ohio Valley and shaped over 10,000 burial mounds. The Serpentine Mound near Hillsboro is more than 1/4th mile long. The lakeside daisy grows in limestone quarries. The state tree is the Buckeye. The state insect is the ladybug.

OKLAHOMA is the Sooner State and it is the 46th in the nation. Will Rogers (1879 to 1935) entertained with rope tricks and witty remarks. He said, "I never met a man I didn't like." Oil is found in every Oklahoma county. There is even an oil pump on the front lawn of the state capitol. Piping plovers nest on sandy river beaches. The Red River's color comes from the clay and minerals in the water. In the 1870s, the Chisholm Trail was a major route to drive cattle north to the Kansas railroads. The National Cowboy Hall of Fame is in Oklahoma City. The state bird is the Scissor tailed Fly Catcher. The state tree is the Redbud. The state wildflower is the Blanketflower. 50,000 settlers moved into Oklahoma overnight. "The Trail of Tears," between 1830 and 1842, was Native Americans who were made to travel over 1,000 miles from the southeast to resettle in Oklahoma.

OREGON is the BEAVER STATE and it is the 33rd in the nation. Oregon harvests more timber than any other state. The northern spotted owl lives in old growth forests. Beavers were once abundant in Oregon waterways. In the 1800s thousands of pelts were used each year to make men's hats. Hell's Canyon on the Snake River is the deepest in the U.S.A. (8,023 feet). The Oregon Trail was a 2,000 mile long wagon trail from Missouri to the Pacific Ocean. Its ruts can still be seen in some places. The state tree is the Douglas Fir. In 1902, the largest meteorite in the U.S.A. was found in Williamette Valley. Crater Lake is the deepest in the U.S.A. (1,932 feet). The state flower is the Oregon Grape. The state bird is the Meadowlark.

PENNSYLVANIA is the Keystone State and the 2nd in the nation. The Declaration of Independence and the U.S. Constitution were written in Philadelphia. It's also home of the Liberty Bell. German settlers called Pennsylvanian Dutch, are still known for simple ways, folk art and farming. Benjamin Franklin, author, inventor, scientist and statesman, lived in Pennsylvania. The state insect is the Firefly. Steel is an important industry. The state tree is the Hemlock. The state flower is the Mountain Laurel. The state bird is the Ruffed Goose.

Steel is an important industry. The Battle of Gettysburg was the turning point in the Civil War. Pennsylvania was the keystone of the original 13 colonies. Northern riffle shell mussels are like streams with the firm packed sand.

RHODE ISLAND is the Ocean State and the 13th in the nation. "The Cradle of American Industry" began at "the place of rushing water" in 1793, when Samuel Slater built a water-powered cotton spinning machine from memory of ones he used in Great Britain. Roger Williams (1603-1683) was befriended by the Massosoit and bought land in 1636 to settle Providence where religious and political freedom were prized. Jewelry and silverware are Rhode Island's leading products. In 1954, Newport held its first jazz festival. It is now world famous. Sailboat races and Navy training are big activities along the Atlantic Coast.

The Rhode Island Red Chicken breed was developed in 1854. Soon the quarry and quantity of eggs and the taste made chicken farming a big industry. The state tree is the red maple. The state flower is the Violet. Loggerhead sea turtles are accidentally caught in shrimp nets while hunting for mollusks, horseshoe crabs and sponges. Providence is the state capital.

SOUTH CAROLINA is the Palmetto State and it is the 8th in the nation. Columbia is the state capital. South Carolina fought 137 battles in the Revolutionary War. Some daring militia hid in swamps to defeat the British in surprise raids. Beautiful beaches and good fishing attract many people to South Carolina. The wood stark is the only true stark in the U.S.A. which dwells in South Carolina. "Peachoid" is a giant water tank in Gaffney built to honor the state's fine peach crops. Excellent banjo and fiddle players come from the Blue Ridge Mountains. The state tree is the Palmetto. In 1776, its logs were used to build a small fort to defeat a British fleet in Charleston Harbor. The state flower is the yellow Jessamine which grows in every corner of the state.

SOUTH DAKOTA is the Mount Rushmore state and it is the 40th in the nation. The capital is Pierre. Sheep were raised in Belle Fourche which produce very strong, white "range wool." The Ring-necked pheasant was introduced from Asia. It is at home in fields and farms in South Dakota. The state flower is the American pasque flower. The state tree is the Black Hills spruce. Boxwork and jewel-like formations grace the walls of wind and jewel caves. Mount Rushmore honors presidents Washington, Jefferson, Theodore Roosevelt and Lincoln. Every fall the Corn Palace in Mitchell is redecorated with corn and multi-colored grain murals. Concerts and dances are held there. The black-footed ferret was once common around prairie dog towns in short-grass prairies.

TENNESSEE is the Volunteer State and it is the 16th in the nation. Davy Crockett was a frontiersman and a gifted storyteller. His motto was "Be always sure you're right. Then go ahead." The Sunsphere Tower at Knoxville's 1982 World's Fair symbolized the Fair's theme, "Energy Turns the World." Tennessee walking horses are raised near Shelbyville and prized for their smooth gait. The state flower is the Iris. The state wildflower is the Passionflower, which was changed to the state wildflower. The state tree is the tulip poplar. . The mockingbird is a talented and varied singer. Reelfoat Lake was created after a violent earthquake in 1811.

TEXAS is the Lone Star state and the 28th in the nation. On May 1, 1981, Henry Cisneros was sworn in as the first Hispanic mayor of a major U.S. city of San Antonio. Texas has many unusual animals. The armadillo protects itself with nine tough armor bands that overlap. In spring, cactus blossoms fill Texas deserts with color. Water sports are popular on the Gulf Coast. Texas leads all states in the production of oil. In 1836, a small army defended a walled mission, the Alamo, in a battle of independence from Mexico. The cry of the Texas Revolution was "Remember the Alamo." Whooping cranes are the tallest birds feeding in marshes. Austin is the state capital. Texas leads the nation in raising beef cattle. The state flower is the Bluebonnet. The state bird is the Mockingbird. The state tree is the pecan. Texas has many unusual animals.

UTAH is the Beehive State. Salt Lake City is the state capital. Southern Utah has many national parks with spectacular arches, spires and canyons. Highlights are "Big Indian" in Monument Valley and Rainbow Bridge National Monument. Brigham Young led the

Mormons from Missouri in search of religious freedom. On July 24, 1847, he first saw the Salt Lake Valley and said, "This is the place." Later, over 4,000 settlers pulled handcarts to Utah. Navajo tribes weave rugs, raise sheep and make turquoise and silver jewelry. Seagulls live on the shores of the Great Salt Lake. Hard-packed salt flats are often where car speed records are set. The Utah prairie dogs live in large colonies called dog towns. The world's first transcontinental railroad joined East to West in Promontory in 1869. The Great Salt Lake is saltier than any ocean, so it's easy to float on it. The state tree is the blue spruce.

VERMONT is the Green Mountain state and it is the 14th in the nation. The state capital is Montpelier. Maple trees are tapped in the late winter to collect maple syrup. Both cross country and downhill skiing are popular in the Vermont Mountains. The state bird is the hermit thrust. The state tree is the Sugar maple. Vermont was the first state after the original 13 colonies to join the union. Vermont citizens come together each March for town meetings to decide local matters. It's a state holiday. Marble and granite are mined in Vermont. Ethan Allen led Vermont's Green Mountain Boys in the American Revolution. His statue, made of Vermont marble, is in Washington D.C. Much electronic equipment is made in Vermont. The state flower is the Red Clover. Vermont is the most rural state in the nation.

VIRGINIA is the Old Dominion and is the 18th state. Mount Vernon was George Washington's home. Richmond is the capital. Eight presidents came from Virginia. They were Washington, Jefferson, Madison, Monroe, William Henry Harrison, Tyler, Taylor and Wilson. The Pentagon is in Virginia. It is five sided. It is one of the largest office buildings in the world and holds U.S. government agencies. The northern flying squirrel can glide over 150 feet through the air. The state tree and the state flower is the Flowering dogwood. The Shenandoah Valley in the Blue Ridge Mountains is a wilderness playground. In 1607, Jamestown was the first permanent American colony. The settlers were seeking gold, but their leader, John Smith, convinced them that surviving was more valuable than hunting for gold. The Norfolk Naval Base is the largest in the U.S.A. Virginia is a center of shipbuilding. Robert E. Lee (1807 to 1870), born in Virginia, led the South in the Civil War because he could not bear to fight against his home state. Chesapeake Bay Bridge is 23 miles long.

WASHINGTON is the Evergreen State. It is the 42nd in the nation. Olympia is the state capital. Tacoma has the world's tallest totem pole which is 105 feet high. Many Pacific Northwest tribes have family or clan emblems on their pole The state flower is the Coast rhododendron in the rain-forest climate of western Washington. Olive Ridley sea turtles mate in the Pacific Ocean. The Space Needle, a tower in Seattle, is 607 feet high. An elevator takes people to see the view from the top. The state tree is the Western hemlock and other evergreens cover half of the state. This state is the only state named after a president. Washington grows more apples than anywhere else in the U.S.A. The state bird is the goldfinch. These "Wild canaries" are found coast to coast. The sockeye and Chinook salmon are born in freshwater rivers and swim to the ocean and return to their birthplace to spawn.

WEST VIRGINIA is the mountain state and it is the 35th in the nation. Homemade quilts, clothes and furniture are traditional. Folk music is very popular and many people still make their own instruments. West Virginia is famous for its pottery, glassware and marbles. In the 1870s, Big Bend Tunnel worker John Henry competed with a steam-powered drill and proved he could work faster than a machine. About 2,000 miles of whitewater provide the best canoeing, kayaking and rafting east of the Mississippi. The cheat mountain salamander lives in moist woodlands. The Rhododendron, the state flower, grows on moist mountain slopes all over West Virginia. The state tree is the Sugar Maple. Charleston is the capital.

WISCONSIN is the Lodger State and the 30th in the nation. Early lead miners lived in caves which they dug into hillsides, much like badgers build their homes. "Americas" Dairy land leads the nation in milk and cheese production. In 1856, Watertown held the first kindergarten class in the U.S.A. Wisconsin has beautiful deep forests. It produces more paper than any other state. Madison is the state capital. There is a scenic river gorge called the Wisconsin Dells. The dwarf lake iris likes sandy soil near the shores of Lake Michigan. The state tree is the Sugar maple which provides shade and syrup. The state bird is the Robin. Every February, Hayward holds the largest cross-country race in the U.S.A. The state flower is the Wood violet.

WYOMING is the Equality State and it is the 44th in the nation. In 1869, Wyoming women were the first to vote. Women in other states had to wait 50 years. Cheyenne is the state capital. The state flower is the Indian paintbrush. The state bird is the Meadowlark. In 1872, before Wyoming was a state, Yellowstone became the first national park. Sheep and cattle graze on more than half the state. The state tree is the cottonwood. The Wyoming toad still lives in a few marshes near the Laramie River. It is one of the rarest amphibians in the world. Frontier Days are celebrations of Wyoming's history, full of rodeos and Native American ceremonies. Yellowstone Lake is the largest high-altitude lake in the U.S.A. It is usually frozen over half of the year. The Great Divide Basin water doesn't flow east or west. It stays where it is. Devils Tower is the core of an ancient volcano and is sacred to many Indian tribes. In 1906 it became the first national monument.

WASHINGTON D.C. is America's Capital City. It became the capital of the U.S.A. in 1800. The president, the nation's chief executive, lives in the White House. The Smithsonian Institution is a museum with over 50 million exhibits. The Capital is where Congress makes laws. The Jefferson Memorial was built to remember our third president, Thomas Jefferson. He was an inspiration for freedom and a great political thinker. He wrote the Declaration of Independence and helped draft the Bill of Rights. In 1912, Japan gave 3,000 white and pink cherry tree saplings to the U.S.A. They grew around the Tidal Basin. The Supreme Court is the highest court in the land. The Lincoln Memorial was built in honor of Abraham Lincoln, one of America's greatest presidents. The District flower is the American beauty rose. The Library of Congress has over 100 million books, manuscripts, films and recordings. The District bird is the Wood thrush. Washington Monument was built in honor of George Washington, America's first president.

—— FIFTY-SEVEN ——

MYTHS AND BELIEFS OF ANCIENT PEOPLE

Myths and ancient beliefs of ancient people existed. The Polynesians lived in a world created by their gods and heroes and they felt a close involvement with them. Simple prayers acknowledged the ever-present gods.

In Hawaii, ordinary men addressed the gods daily before the meal. The translation is by W.V. Westervelt. "O long god, O short god, O god breathing in short sibilant breaths, O god blowing like the whistling, winds! O god watching, peeping at one! O god hiding, slipping out of sight. O all ye gods who travel on the dark nights paths! Come and eat!"

Men also needed more specialized assistance to communicate with their gods. All labor was consecrated. The success of planting, fishing, canoe making and house-building depended not only on correct technique but also on correct ritual. Priests, shamans and other early tribesmen and tribeswomen taught their followers technical skills and his collection of spells, invocations, genealogies and legends. The highest mysteries of traditional lore were the province of the divine chief, the inspiration priest and the ceremonial priest.

Every Polynesian chief traced his genealogy back to the gods and the mythological past. The inspirational priest was the mouthpiece of the gods, the oracle and diviner, who was consulted before any event of importance.

Chanting, singing and dancing took place in almost every early tribe with ceremonial rituals and reciting of ancient beliefs. They rubbed themselves with colorful paints, dyes and perfumed oils and adorned themselves with feather ruffs, anklets and hair ornaments and wore bark garments.

The Arioi was essentially a cult organization like the ghost and spirit societies of Melanesia. The Arioi of the Society Islands were united by the great rock-of-the-Arioi. Their dances were performed to stimulate fertility. They prayed to their spirit gods. They served at public ceremonies like the festival of the first fruits for the god Lono, Laka, the goddess of the wildwood and sister of Lono, was their patroness.

Among the Polynesians genesis was conceived of as either a process of growth or evolution from an intangible to a tangible state, or as the work of a preexistent, omniscient creator who brought matter into existence, gave form to the formless and set all in an established order. The belief in a pre-existent creator called Tangaloa, who lived alone in the Illimitable Void and made all things, was found in the western Polynesian islands of the Samoan, Tongan and Ellice groups and on Nueie, Uvea and Rotuma. Tangaloa some said, brooded over a vast expanse of waters while his messenger, the bird Tuli, flew over the never-ending oceans searching for somewhere to rest. At last Tangaloa cast down a rock which became the island of Mau'a, the main island of the Samoan group.

Next, he made the other islands of the group, then Tonga and Fiji. Tuli complained of the lack of shade in those islands and Tangaloa gave him a vine to plant called the Peeping Vine, from which man was made. The Maori view of creation in which all nature was seen as a great kinship tracing its origins back to a single pair, the Sky Father and the Earth Mother, was a conception which they brought with them when they came from central Polynesia about 1,000 A.D. Furthermore, the belief in a primal pair as well as the metaphysical idea of an original Void or Darkness seems to be part of the stock of ideas which the ancestors of the Polynesians brought with them from the west, from the Asian mainland and which they carried with them as they dispersed into marginal Polynesia.

The Sky Father, known as Rangi by the Tuomotuans and Atea, which means "Great expanse of sky or light," was the name most commonly given in eastern Polynesia. The male force was also known as Te Tumu, the source or cause. Papa, which means Earth foundation, and was the most usual name for the Earth Mother but sometimes, especially on coral atolls like those of the Tuomotuan chain, the female element was known as Fakahoto or Hakshotu, names which suggest coral growth.

Although the Mangoian islanders of the Cook group believed that Vatea (Atea) and Papa were the progenitors of gods and men, they did not know Vatea as the Sky Father but as one of the six children which Varma-te-takers, the Beginning-and-the-bottom, plucked from her side. He was formed half-fish, half-man. The Marquesians believed that the universe was contained within a vast coconut shell called Avaiki (Hawaiki) and the very bottom dwelt Vari, a self-existent being.

Below Vari, and contained within the tapered point of the stem of the coconut was the threadlike Root-of-all-existence. Tane and the whale universe was said to be constantly sustained from that point. Above Vari were the various strata allocated to gods and men.

The idea of an initial kernel of life being enclosed within a spherical, primal form is found elsewhere in Polynesia. Sometimes it is represented as an egg; sometimes as a shell.

Ta-aroa's supremacy over the other gods, particularly Tane, was constantly stressed. At Tane's birth the question was asked, "Did you notice whom he resembles?" The reply was, "A clod of earth. A huge jellyfish. A shapeless nothing."

It was Ta'aroa who summoned the artisans with their baskets of adzes to fashion him into "a good-looking boy." Again it was Ta'aroa who exalted Tane and gave him the tenth or highest heaven as his dwelling place. Tane retained the leading part however in raising the skies and this version of the myth provides one of the most colorful elaborations of this theme.

That god took his basket of flashing shell adzes and his pet white swallow, and descended to Earth. He used great logs as props and levers and began to bore into Atea with his shells. Atea cried out in pain but Tane went on digging and boring until at least Atea was freed and light came into the world. There was a rolling and tumbling as the gods fell over themselves with joy at their release. The arms of the octopus became detached and fell away to become the island of Tabuai' in the Austral group.

The above beliefs were important to the early Polynesian people. They focused on their gods and spirits.

The Mayan nation had its beliefs and myths. The creation of the Earth was told this way. "In the beginning everything was still, peaceful and silent. There was no movement because the whole expanse of the sky was empty. There were no people, no animals, no birds, fish, crabs, rocks, ravines and no mountains. Only the sky was there, completely empty. The Earth still did not exist and there was nothing that could make a sound.

Everything was in silence and the sea was there, motionless in the darkness. Only the Creators and Makers Tepew and Q'uk'umatz were above the waters, surrounded by light and covered with green and blue feathers. They were wise man and great thinkers because they were the helpers of the Heart of Heaven, which is the name of God. Tepew and Q'uk'umatz met together. They joined their words and thoughts and decided to create the trees and the vines. By the will of the Heart of Heaven, also known as Juragan, they created plants out of the darkness and gave life to humans. This myth about the creation of the Earth is strongly believed by the Mayans of K'iche'.

There were many myths and beliefs which existed during the days of the ancient civilizations. These people were believers in primitive creations.

The Mayans had many myths and beliefs. More of their myths were about the creation of animals, the creation of humans known as the clay people and the wooden people. Other stories and myths are "The Pride of Wuqub' K'aqix (Seven Macaws), Sipakna the Mountain Giant, the Death of Sipakna, Kab'raqan, Lord of the Earthquakes, Jun Junajpu and Wugub' Junajpu, the first Set of Twins and the Xib'alb'a Lords, Princess Ixkik, Princess Ixkik' Passes the Test, The Birth of Junaipu and Ixb 'alanke, the Amazing Twins, How the Amazing Twins Became Ball Players, The Messenger Creatures, The Journey to Xib'alb'a, The Tests of Xib'alb'a, The

Death and Resurrection of Junajpu and Ixb'alonke, the Third Creation of Humans---The Corn People and the Gift of Fire.

The first Fathers of the K'iche' Nation is about the Founding of the Tribes, The Death of the First Fathers and Genealogy of the Kiche' Kings. The Mayans believed in Nature spirits and elemental spirits of fire, air and earth. Their myths, beliefs and legends were created over hundreds of years. THE POPOL VUH is the Sacred Book of the Bible of the Maya Kiche', which is the literary gem of the indigenous people of Guatemala.

— FIFTY-EIGHT —

TEACHING PIANO

Knowing how to teach piano requires awareness of how to learn to play the piano step by step. There are white and black keys. Beginning piano students learn the middle C up to higher C and middle C to lower C first. They learn two octaves. Then they continue to expand their awareness of more octaves above and below middle C.

Black notes are above the white keys. Black notes are sharps and flats. Sharps are ½ step to the right of the white notes. Flats are ½ step to the left of the regular notes. All notes played must be recognized before and while they are played. Many notes in different octaves must be learned and played with precision and immediate recognition.

Once the essential white and black notes are learned piano students learn different rhythms such as 4/4 time, 3/4 time, 2/4 time, etc. They learn to interpret piano pieces by playing loudly and softly and in between in each piano piece. Interpretation of music is important.

Many notes must be learned step by step. Notes are repeated over and over until they are learned. Students of piano must learn to identify each note and locate the piano keys which are to be played according to specific notes.

Piano students learn by grade levels. Beginning piano books are used. Then piano students continue in Grade One, Grade Two, Grade Three and they continue to play in Grade Four and then Grade Five. Students who become more advanced piano players continue in Grade Six and Seven.

To learn to play the piano requires concentration, discipline and regular practice time. Excellent piano players are able to play a variety of pieces from classical to jazz. Classical piano pieces are available composed by Beethoven, Mozart, Debussy, Chopin, Hayden, Bartok, Grieg, Lizyt, Tchaikovsky and many others.

Jazz piano pieces have a certain rhythm and style which is different than classical music. It is important to learn different types of piano pieces to be a well rounded pianist.

Piano students usually perform in piano recitals, piano competitions and other community events. They can perform in church and at school. Individuals who learn to play the piano are able to perform in musicals and in peoples' homes and community centers. It is worthwhile to learn to play the piano.

Piano teachers should use a variety of techniques when they are teaching different age groups. Piano teachers should review the keyboard step by step with each piano student. They should teach their students to play rhythmically and accurately. Piano teachers should use effective piano books to teach piano. Effective piano techniques help piano students to become better pianists.

—— FIFTY-NINE ——

ASTRONAUTS GO TO THE MOON

The NASA program has been creating rockets and spacecraft to travel into outer space. Neil Armstrong, Buzz Aldren and Scott Carpenter traveled to the Moon on July 20, 1969.

Before the flight the astronauts prepared for the challenges of outer space travels. They all had to be in top physical shape. The astronauts were trained to endure space travel. They had to get used to certain foods which they would eat in the spacecraft.

On July 20, 1969, Neil Armstrong, Buzz Aldren and Scott Carpenter boarded a NASA rocket. They sat in their assigned seats dressed in astronaut rocket suits. They prepared for take off.

After the countdown the NASA rocket took off. NASA employees were sitting at computers and were observing the NASA rocket. They were able to communicate with the three astronauts while they were in outer space.

As the NASA rocket approached the Moon, Neil Armstrong, Buzz Aldren and Michael Collins prepared to land on the Moon. As the rocket came close to the Moon the astronauts had difficulty landing the rocket safely. The rocket almost crashed on the Moon. The astronauts used a stick device to land the rocket.

Once the NASA rocket finally landed Neil Armstrong and Buzz Aldren stepped out on the Moon. Neil Armstrong said, "This is one small step for mankind." The American flag was placed on the Moon. The astronauts explored around the Moon. Michael Collins remained overhead in the orbital spacecraft. Then the two astronauts stepped back into the NASA rocket. They tried to leave the Moon. The NASA rocket wouldn't budge. Finally, Neil Armstrong used an ink pen to turn on the rocket. It finally lifted off the Moon.

The NASA rocket returned to the larger spacecraft. The astronauts returned to the Earth safely. President Nixon announced the success of the space flight to the Moon and back to the Earth. President Nixon stated this July 20, 1969 space flight marked the fact that this was the first time astronauts had landed on the Moon and returned successfully to the Earth.

Other astronauts have attempted to travel into outer space since this first space flight. More and more space flights have occurred since that historic space flight.

—— SIXTY ——

LEARN ABOUT CENTRAL AMERICA

GUATEMALA

GUATEMALA is called The Land of Eternal Spring. This is the northern most Central American country. The erogenous people of Guatemala are known as the ladinos. Many in this group are descendents of the Spanish who colonized the country in the sixteenth and seventeenth centuries. Traditionally this group is more educated than the native Guatemalans and occupies nearly all position of power in the nation.

Guatemala has beautiful and contrasting geographies. Guatemala has black sand beaches, volcanic peaks and cactus-studded deserts. The northern region of Guatemala is between Mexico to the west and Belize to the east and is known as the Peten. The Peten is inhabited by spider monkeys, wild pigs, jaguars and a variety of exotic birds. Heavy rainfall seeps through the porous limestone and collects in lakes in underground caverns. These lakes are called cenotes.

The ancient Maya drew from these freshwater reserves for drinking water. Archaeologists have found ceramic pieces and precious stones in these underground lakes. Mayans made ceremonial offerings to them.

The Peten is the most sparsely populated and least developed region of Guatemala. However, between the years A.D. 250 and A.D. 830, Mayan civilization flourished in the Peten. At the height of Mayan civilization, the region was one of the most densely populated in history. Almost 2,600 people per square mile in the cities and up to 1,300 people per square mile in rural areas. In comparison, New York City today has a population density of only 2,300 people per square mile.

For today's standards the land of the Peten is not fully understood how the Maya managed to support such a large population for so long. Within one hundred years two-thirds of the population had disappeared from the Peten. This decline continued for centuries.

Mayan temples and other trappings of civilization were covered with forests so they were hidden. By 1970 a road was built that could accommodate heavy traffic. As a result, Peten has become one of the fastest growing regions of Central America. Immigrants now arrive at a rate of three hundred or more a week

Most of the new arrivals are farmers, loggers and cattle ranchers who reduce the subtropical forest by as much as 100,000 acres a year. Consequently this area is once again being systematically deforested. What remains of the Petens rainforest hides many archaeological sites. Eighty sites that have been discovered are considered highly important by archaeologists.

Tikal is one of these important archeological sites, which stands as one of the most impressive collections of ancient buildings in Central America. Tikal spans ten square miles and includes temples, plazas, causeways and many other structures. Excavations and restoration is a full time job at Tikal. Although thousands of individual structures have already been unearthed, it is believed that thousands of structures still lie in the ground.

Guatemalan farmers plant coffee as the highland region's main crop. The central Sierra Madre mountain range, running roughly east and west, cuts across Guatemala.

Periodic eruptions of Guatemala's volcanoes have produced rich soil that is ideal for growing the region's main crop, coffee. Guatemalan coffee growers employ a method of cultivation that was developed in the late 1800s. Indigenous trees shade the coffee plants, which need filtered sunlight in order to produce a superior quality of coffee. Guatemalan shade-grown coffee is considered among the finest in the world.

A valley high in the central highlands is the home of Guatemala City, the nation's capital. Guatemala City is a modern metropolis and serves as the country's economic and cultural center. Guatemala City was founded on the first day of 1776, after Guatemala's original colonial capital at Antigua was destroyed by a series of devastating earthquakes. The greatest challenge for Guatemala City has been rapid population growth driven by difficult economic times in the countryside.

The original architect of Guatemala City laid out the settlement in the classical Spanish style grid around a central plaza. This city faces serious shortages of electricity, water, public transportation, police protection and other necessary services.

The contrast between rich and poor is great in Guatemala City. The wealthier residents live in gated suburban communities, while most of the city's middle class live in boxlike houses in the inner city. The native peasants live in shantytowns consisting of shacks made of plywood, cardboard or plastic. These communities lack the benefit of clean water supplies or sewage systems.

Antigua is southwest of Guatemala City. Antigua is a picturesque colonial town with cobblestone streets and the Agua volcano above this place. Nearby is Lake Atilan, which British author Aldus Huxley once called the world's most beautiful lake. Three volcanoes surround this lake and its shore is dotted with a dozen indigenous villages. With depths of one thousand feet, Lake Atitlan is the deepest lake in the Western Hemisphere.

The residents of the Caribbean coast are largely of African descent and are known as Garifuna. The Garifuna, descendants of African slaves brought to the

Americas in the seventeenth and eighteenth centuries are culturally distinct from the Maya. The Garifuna spread out along the Caribbean to Belize, Guatemala and Honduras intermarrying with the Maya. Because of their mixture of African and Caribbean heritage, the Garifuna have a unique mixture of cultural characteristics that include circular dances, banana cultivation, rooster and pig sacrifices. Their ways of food production are still based in subsistence farming and fishing. The Garifuna speak a language that is also called Garifuna, a mixture of French and indigenous languages, Creole, Bambu and Patua.

Puerto Barrios is the primary metropolitan area of Guatemala's Caribbean coast. The city lies near an area of extensive banana cultivation. The United Fruit Company built Puerto Barrios in the early twentieth century as a port from which to ship its bananas. This company also built a series of railway lines from the interior to Puerto Barrios.

For almost two thousand years the land that would become Guatemala was home to one of the most advanced civilizations in the ancient world. The people known today as the Maya constructed elaborate cities in the jungles of the highlands and the Peten. From the fourth through the tenth century A.D., a time when Europe was in a Dark Age, the Maya were using advanced forms of geometry to design structures such as the great Plaza in Tikal. Mayan mathematicians were able to predict with precision the movements of the sun, moon and planets. Mayan scientists developed a calendar more accurate than even the one in general use today. Mayan scholars developed works of art, literature and philosophy. They developed one of the earliest recorded written languages and set down their history in stone carvings and long paper tablets. They had a highly developed religion that venerated the sun, the moon and other celestial objects as gods.

The Maya developed farming and irrigation techniques essential for supporting their population. They traded through north to central Mexico and south into modern day Panama. Mayan cities flourished across the Central American region. The Maya did not have a central government. It had priest-kings who ruled over individual city-states. These priest-kings were considered divine beings who were entitled to obedience, tribute and manpower from the people they ruled.

As advanced as Mayan civilization was, by A.D. 950 political strife, civil war and famine had brought Mayan dominance in the region to an end. The lack of unity among the Mayan tribes made them an easy target for outsiders to conquer. The Spanish arrived in 1523 with enormous military power using gunpowder, steel swords and horses. By 1525 Pedro de Albarado from Spain defeated the main highland tribes. The first Utalans, the Tzutujil on the shores of Lake Astitlan, the Pipil tribe and the Mam were conquered after a siege of their capital, Zaculeu. In 1527 Alvarado established the first permanent Spanish settlement in Guatemala which is at Ciudad Vieja.

Spain lacked interest in Guatemala so the Mayan culture managed to survive the Spanish conquest. Elsewhere in the Americas, the lure of gold and silver caused exploitation by the conquistadors. The Spanish experienced little opposition to their rule in Guatemala. So, they had no reason to destroy the Mayan culture as they had in Mexico and Peru. Spanish rule was harsh. Indians had no rights and were forced to perform hard labor such as building churches and administrative buildings for little or no pay. Diseases brought by the Spanish ravaged the native populations. Mayan people dropped by ninety percent or more during the first century of Spanish rule and population recovery was slow and sporadic for centuries.

By the early nineteenth century a desire for independence had developed not just in Guatemala but throughout Central America. By 1821 Spain finally granted freedom to Guatemala and throughout Central America. By 1821 Spain finally granted freedom to Guatemala without a fight. By 1873 President Justo Rufino Barrias Auyon developed the nation economically.

In modern times, products such as Coca Cola have become an everyday part of life for the Mayans who have moved to the cities. There is new interest in Mayan studies programs at universities around the world. Mayan women earn money weaving traditional clothing which is sold to tourists and even to customers over the Internet. The Mayans are mostly farmers. Traditionally they view the land as something sacred. Indians consider themselves not so much owners as caretakers of land.

Most of the women and the men still wear brightly colored native dress. Men usually work in the field. While women care for the children and weave textiles with motifs that are unique to each community. Mayans construct their homes with wooden poles set in a stone foundation. Two doorways are placed directly opposite each other to allow for the free flow of air. The framework is rounded and filled in with additional poles or with stucco. The entire home is topped by a thick palm-thatched roof. Sometimes cinder blocks and cement are used as well as corrugated metal or tar and paper roofing.

The Garifuna celebration is a sacred festival called dugu which means "family reunion "involving relatives both living and deceased. The dugu begins with burning of a fragrant resin, copal which provides a scent to cleanse the ritual area. Drums are played and women dance until they go into "oniwishant", a trancelike state. Once in this state they sing messages from ancestors to other family members. Traditionally the Garifuna also believe they can direct the forces of good and evil through spells. These rituals and spells underscore the Garifuna's West African and Indian traditions with some elements of Catholicism mixed in.

Young Garifuna prefer to fish instead of farming. There are a small professional class of teachers, nurses and civil servants among the Garifuna. In Garifuna society, few couples mark their unions with legal or religious ceremonies. Grandparents often take care of their grandchildren. Males are expected to leave their parents' home, find jobs and support their families.

Ladinos dominate the economic and cultural life in Guatemala. Most Ladinos are of European descent. However, a Ladino many be a full blooded Indian, who has assimilated and adopted Ladino culture. Ladinos wear European and American-style clothing and live mostly in urban areas. Spanish is their primary language. Ladinos also dominated political life in Guatemala.

Religion is an important part of life in Guatemala. Guatemala celebrates traditional Catholic holidays with large public festivals. Every village and city devotes a celebration to its own patron saint. These days are celebrated fireworks, music and processions through the streets. One large festival is the Feria de Jocotonango held in Guatemala City in honor of the Virgin Mary.

HONDURAS

Honduras is southeast of Guatemala in Central America. Honduras is filled with high mountains, misty forests, thick jungles and pristine beaches. Honduras is a mixture of indigenous peoples, Spanish conquerors and African slaves. There are monkeys, jaguars, sloths, scarlet macaws and toucans. The brightly colored beak of the teal-billed toucan grows up to 8 inches long.

Copan was an ancient city which was once home to twenty thousand people. Spain ruled Honduras for hundreds of years. Honduras finally became independent from Spain. Military leaders, frequent battles with neighboring countries and interference by foreign governments weakened the struggling country.

By the end of the nineteenth century foreign banana companies were taking advantage of Honduran workers, leading the country further into poverty. The Hondurans would not give up. They demanded free elections and workers' rights. Because of their long fight, Honduras has been democratic for more than twenty years. Labor unions have been established, protecting factory and plantation workers. Hondurans remain proud of their past. Today, they are working to restore Copan, one of the great Mayan cities, to its former glory. They are also proud of their present. They are conserving their forests and jungles which they consider national treasures.

Honduras is shaped like a large triangle. Its northern coast borders the Caribbean Sea, while its southern coast borders the Pacific Ocean.

Honduras also includes the Bay Islands located in the Caribbean Sea and islands in the Gulf of Fonseca in the Pacific Ocean.

Historians claim that Christopher Columbus discovered Honduras when his ship experienced a violent storm. Christopher Columbus steered his ship up to what is now Trujillo, Honduras in 1502.

More than three-fourths of Honduras is covered with mountains, the most of any Central American country. Swift rivers zigzag through the mountains pine and rain forests. Several wide, level valleys called basins cut through the mountains. Pico Bonito in Northern Honduras soars 7,992 feet into the sky. In the basins beans, cattle, coffee and corn are raised. One of the most important basins is the Comayagua Valley. Vegetables such as tomatoes, peppers, squash and eggplants are grown there for export to the United States and Asia.

The second largest city in Honduras is San Pedro Sula which lies in the northwestern part of the country. It is the nation's most industrial and commercial city and is the center of manufacturing and trade. Industries include concrete, shoes, plastics, steel and textiles. One of the best museums in the country, the Museum of Anthropology and History, is located in San Pedro Sula. In 2005, the city had an estimated population of 489,466.

Comayagua, the most important city of the colonial Honduras, was founded in 1537. In 1880, Tegucigalpa was named the permanent capital of Honduras. La Ceiba, Honduran's third largest city, is located along the Caribbean coast at the base of the soaring mountain called Pico Bonito, It is the commercial center for the Standard Fruit Company, which grows pineapples and bananas.

On the Pacific coastal plain, cotton, melons and sugarcane are grown. Cattle are also raised there. The Cholutera River enters the Pacific Ocean in the Gulf of Fonseca. Most local people fish for a living. Shrimp farming has become an important business. Honduras' third largest port, Puerto Henecan, is on the Pacific Coast.

Several islands located in the Gulf of Foneca are part of Honduras. The two largest islands are Isla del Tigre and Isla Zacate Grande. They are ancient volcanoes that are no longer active. There is more human activity on Honduras' Caribbean coast than on the Pacific Coast. Its rich river valleys make excellent farmland to grow pineapples, lemons, oranges, sugarcane and bananas which are sold locally as well as exported. Puerto Cortes, the main port of Honduras and Puerto Castilla, the second, largest port, are both on the Caribbean Coast.

The Bay Islands have been visited by Spanish conquistadores, slave traders, indigenous peoples and pirates. Today, divers from all over the world visit Bay Islands to explore the pristine coral reef off its shores where colorful fish thrive.

The largest lake is Lake Yajoa. The longest coastline is the Caribbean Sea Coast which is 382 miles long. The longest river is Coco River which is 485 miles long. The greatest annual rainfall is 100 inches in the Caribbean coastal region. The lowest annual rainfall is 30 inches in the central highlands.

Most rivers in Honduras flow into the Caribbean Sea. Honduras' second longest river is the Patuca, which has a dramatic waterfall and is surrounded by densely forested mountains. The Ulua River and Chamelicon River converge, flowing into the northern Sula Valley. On the Pacific Coast, the Chaluteca, Nacaome and Goascoran rivers flow into the ocean. Lake Yojon, the largest lake is located between the capital, Tegucigalpa and San Pedro Sula. Lake Yogjoa is home to more than 373 species of birds. Three national parks have been set up in the lake area to help protect the wildlife. Lake Yagoa is famous for its bird watching and bass fishing.

There are two seasons in Honduras. The dry season runs from November through April and the rainy season runs from May to October. Honduras is generally warm year-round. However, the temperature can change and fluctuate widely.

Honduras suffers frequent hurricanes. Hurricanes attacked Honduras in 1969, 1982, 1974 and 1998. The coastal lowlands are warm and humid. The average temperature throughout the year is about 88 degrees. In the mountains the average temperature is 74 degrees.

Rain falls throughout the year. The Pacific coast experiences high temperatures but has a drier climate than the Caribbean coast.

Honduras has three types of monkeys. They are spider monkeys, white faced capuchins and howler monkeys. The howler monkey gets its name from its loud call which can be heard up to 3 miles away. Its neck and jaw are large, to support its big vocal chords.

Jaguars will hunt almost any kind of animal, including wild pigs, cattle, snakes and fish. White-faced capuchins are smart and lively. Fruit such as mangoes, guavas and papayas are the mainstay of their diet. Honduras' national mammal is the Yucatan whitetailed deer. This deer can be found both on the country's plains and in its pine forests.

There are armadillos, raccoons, opossums and agoutis that thrive on the ground in Honduras. An agouti is a rodent that is related to the guinea pig. When the agouti first senses danger it freezes. It sits upright and then lets out a sharp scream while scampering away. The agouti is a common prey for the jaguar.

Cougars and jaguars live deep in the jungle. Coatis, which are related to raccoons, climb from branch to branch in troops of up to twenty. Iguanas live in the jungle. Hondurans catch iguanas to make a nice meal. To catch an iguana, a banana is placed on a hook and put out as a lure. When the iguana bites the banana, it is caught on the hook like a fish.

The largest mammal native to Honduras is the Baird's tapir. Almost the size of a donkey, the Baird's tapir weighs up to 800 pounds. Its nose looks like a pig's snout. It uses its snout to stuff leaves into its small mouth. This mammal lives near water. They rush to water to escape from danger.

Domestic animals in Honduras are cows, horses, donkeys, goats and oxen. Oxen are used to pull wagons or carts filled with goods. Cats and dogs are family pets. Chicken are raised to eat. There are mosquitoes, sand flies and blue morpho butterflies. Honduras has fer-de-lance and coral snakes. Several types of vipers include the eyelash viper, the jumping viper and the rain forest hog-nosed viper which are venomous.

Honduras is home to a vast array of brightly colored birds. More than seven hundred different bird species live in Honduras. These include woodpeckers, robins, jays, quails, ducks, cuckoos, parakeets, hummingbirds, toucans, oropendolas, parrots, quetzals, green toucans and scarlet macaws.

Off the Bay Islands is the Mesoamerican Reef, the world's second largest coral reef. Many types of sharks prowl the waters near this reef. The whale shark is the largest fish in the world. It can grow to lengths of almost 60 feet and can weigh over 20 tons. It feeds on plankton and small fish.

Small, colorful fish such as butterflyfish, yellowtail snapper and angelfish swim near the shore. Hidden in the coral reefs are seahorses, octopi, sea turtles, eels, eagle rays, manta rays, mackerels, tunas, marlins and kingfish live in the ocean.

Honduras' plants are red and white pine, oak and maple trees dominate the mountain slopes. Much coffee is grown in the mountains of Honduras. The national flower is the rose. Coffee makes up about a fifth of all Honduran exports. Mahogany, strangler fig, oak and rosewood are common in wet forests.

Honduras has thirteen national parks. The park's mountains are filled with dense vegetation that blocks the sun's rays. Water drips from towering trees covered with ferns, vines and moss. The northern coast consists of grassland and swamps along with palm and pine forests. This also is the banana-growing area of Honduras. The soil is rich and the climate is hot and damp which is perfect for banana crops. Bananas were brought hundreds of years ago from Africa by the Portuguese. Cacao trees also grow in the area. The large, oval fruit pod grows from the trunk or branches of the tree. The Maya believes that cacao was brought directly to the Earth by the gods. Cacao trees flower two or three times a year. Once ripe, the pods are cracked open to collect twenty to sixty thin-skinned seeds; Chocolate is made from the processed seeds.

The Maya had one of the greatest civilizations in the Americas. The Mayan world spread across what is now southern Mexico, Belize, Guatemala and El Salvador. By the fifth century A.D., Mayan civilization had reached western Honduras. There the Maya built a city called Copan. This city was filled with temples and pyramids. In time, Copan became a center of Mayan culture. At Copan, the Maya carved statues of their rulers and other important people.

EL SALVADOR

El Salvador is the smallest country in Central America. It is slightly smaller than the U.S. state of Massachusetts. El Salvador's land is varied. San Salvador is the capital of El Salvador.

People call the volcano Izalco the Lighthouse of the Pacific. El Salvador is often called the land of volcanoes. This country has several active volcanoes, such as Izalco and San Miguel. The tallest, active volcano is Santa Ana. It stands 7,757 feet high.

El Salvador declared its independence on September 15, 1821. On this day, El Salvador and four other Central American colonies split from Spain. The other colonies were Costa Rica, Guatemala, Honduras and Nicaragua. The five colonies joined the Mexican Empire. People in El Salvador were not happy. They did not want to be ruled by the Mexican Empire. They wanted freedom.

In 1823, El Salvador and the other four colonies broke from the Mexican Empire. They formed the United Provinces of Central America. In 1844, El Salvador split itself from this group. El Salvador's government is a republic. Like the United States of America, El Salvador has an executive and a legislative branch. El Salvador's government meets in San Salvador, the capital city.

Salvadorans elect a president and a vice president for a term of five years. Manuel Jose Arce served as the first president of the United Provinces of Central America. In 2004, Elias Antonio Saca was elected president.

People live in many different kinds of houses in El Salvador. Outside the cities, some people live in houses made out of adobe. The poorest people build huts with tree branches covered with mud. 58 percent of the people live in urban areas. 42 percent of the people live in the rural areas. In the cities, many people live in small tin or cardboard houses. Others live in apartments and small houses.

Rich Salvadorans own houses. Some of the rich live in or near the cities. Others live on large, coffee plantations in the country.

Salvadorans travel by bus. Many people also walk from place to place. In large cities, people can ride in taxis. Visitors to El Salvador often arrive by airplane. El Salvador has one international airport near San Salvador.

El Salvador has good city highways and roads. Roads outside the cities are often in poor shape. In the 1970s, Salvadorans fought for land and jobs which led to a long civil war. The war damaged the country. Many roads have not been fixed since then. People use a cart and oxen on unpaved roads.

Farming is El Salvador's main industry. El Salvador's soil and climate are good for growing coffee beans. Farmers also grow cotton and sugarcane.

El Salvador is working to add new businesses. Factories now make clothing and furniture. They also make rubber goods and medicines. Schools in El Salvador are open from January through October. Children must go to school from ages 7 to 12. They can attend public schools for free. Some Salvadoran families pay for their children to go to a private school. Religious groups run these schools. Children in El Salvador study Math, History and Geography. They also take computer classes and physical education classes.

El Salvador does not have enough teachers or schools. Many children leave school to work. Others cannot afford school supplies. El Salvador is working hard to improve its public schools.

Salvadorans play soccer, basketball, go horseback riding or play tennis and golf. People in El Salvador enjoy their free time. Many people get together to fish and go swimming. Young children play hopscotch and marbles.

Salvadorans make crafts from natural materials. People weave palm leaves into brooms and baskets. Some people use seeds and beads to make jewelry such as necklaces and bracelets. They use wood to make toys and furniture. Artists are found in many Salvadoran cities. Potters in Tlabasco are famous for their ceramic figures. Artists in La Palma are known for the colorful designs they paint on wood, ceramics and jewelry.

Many holidays in El Salvador are religious celebrations. The first week of August is the Feast of the Holy Savior, El Salvador's patron saint. People get together for parades, music and food. Towns also hold festivals for their own patron saints. Christmas is also a weeklong celebration in El Salvador. Families have nightly posadas or parades. They go to church on Christmas Eve. Children receive gifts. Other holidays are Columbus Day, New Year's Day and Teachers Day. September 15 is Independence Day. People celebrate the day El Salvador became free from Spain. Many people have time off from work and school. They watch parades and have family picnics.

Salvadorans cook traditional foods with corn, beans and rice. They use corn flour to make flat, round bread called tortillas. Tortillas are folded and filled with stewed or fried beans called frijoles. Cooks may add rice, vegetables and meat. Street merchants in El Salvador sell pupusas. Pupusas are small cornmeal pancakes. They are filled with soft white cheese, refried beans and pork rinds.

Tamales are corn dough wrapped and cooked in banana leaves with meat added. Many foods are available to people in the cities. Markets sell fresh meats, fish, fruits and vegetables.

Family is the center of Salvadoran life. Most families are large with four or more children. Children and their parents may live with grandparents, aunts and uncles. Before El Salvador's civil war, women stayed home to care for their family. Men helped with farm work and other jobs. El Salvador's civil war weakened the country. It also hurt families. Now both parents often hold jobs. Many men cannot find work near home. They must leave their families to find work in other cities. Some of the cities are Santa Ana, Sonsonate, Acajutla, La Libertad, Ilobasco, San Miguel, La Union as well as the capital, San Salvador and La Palma.

Until 2001, El Salvador's money was the colon. In January 2001, El Salvador began using the U.S. dollar as well as the colon. The government hoped to bring world business to El Salvador. In 2004, one U.S. dollar equaled 8.75 colons. The El Salvadoran flag has three stripes. The blue stripes stand for unity. The white stripes stand for peace. In the middle of the white stripe is the national coat of arms. The triangle on the coat of arms stands for equality.

NICARAGUA

Nicaragua is another country in Central America which is a little smaller than Louisiana in America. To the north of Nicaragua lies Honduras and to the south is

Costa Rica. Large areas of Nicaragua are still uninhabited. Nicaragua is covered with forests, lakes, mountains and volcanoes. Nicaragua is surrounded by the Pacific Ocean and Caribbean Sea. This country's population per square mile is relatively thin compared to other Central American countries.

Earthquakes and volcanic eruptions are frequent occurrences in Nicaragua. Nicaragua is divided into three geographic regions which are the western Pacific lowlands, the central highlands and the eastern Caribbean lowlands called the Mosquito Coast. In the Pacific lowlands three out of four Nicaraguans live in the western part of the country between the Pacific coast and Lake Managua. The land has been enriched to grow crops. Many of the people who live here work on farms. Nicaragua's three biggest cities, Leon, Managua and Granada are also in this region. The largest is Managua, the nation's capital. East of Managua is the area known as the central highlands. This mountainous area is covered with dense rain forests and receives an annual rainfall of between 70 and 100 inches. This is an inspiring beautiful land of coffee plantations and cool, misty forests. In the northern mountains is a rich mining district called Nueva Segovia. Few people do mining of silver and gold.

The Mosquito Coast runs along the eastern third of the country. This region is the wettest area in Central America with average annual rainfall ranging from 100 to 250 inches with gravel and sandy clay and treeless grassy plain called savanna. This area was named after the Miskito people, who have lived here for centuries. When the Spanish name, Costa Miskito, the other main groups, who live here are the Rama and Sumo, who are natives of Nicaragua and the Garifuna, who were originally from Africa. These groups have lived in this swamp-like region for many generations. Many build their houses on stilts for protection from floods and snakes.

Few Nicaraguans travel between the Pacific Coast and the Mosquito Coast. Only a few roads link the two sides of the country, so travel is mostly by plane and boast. A network of waterways throughout Nicaragua play an important role in the country's system of transportation, commerce and daily life.

The best farmland is near the lakes, rivers and seas. Rivers mark the boundaries between Nicaragua and its neighbors Honduras and Costa Rica. Nicaragua has two large lakes known as Lake Managua and Lake Nicaragua. Lake Nicaragua's historic name is Lake Cocibolca and it is 45 miles wide and 110 miles long. It has three volcanoes and over 300 islands, mostly inhabited. Lake Nicaragua is Central America's largest lake and the world's tenth largest freshwater lake. There are freshwater sharks. Rio Tipitapa connects this lake to Lake Managua, which covers 390 square miles.

Volcanoes are largely responsible for the geographic makeup of Nicaragua. Many lakes and islands were formed by volcanic activity. Cities developed near the volcanoes because fertile farmland there attracted early settlers. At least a dozen active volcanoes and many more dormant ones give the landscape a beautiful quality.

Nicaragua's government is optimistic about using the country's abundant geothermal resources to reduce their need for imported oil. A geothermal plant near the Momotombo volcano, about 50 miles from Managua, generates nonpolluting energy using the steam that rises from the depths of the volcano. There are plans to build more geothermal plants in Nicaragua in the near future.

Nicaragua suffers from other natural calamities such as droughts, tsunamis and hurricanes. Managua, the capital, is located about 87 degrees west of the prime meridian and lies about 12 degrees north of the equator. Nicaragua has a tropical climate. It is warm in the morning, hot and humid in the afternoon and pleasant at night. The warm climate is a good place for monkeys, alligators and snakes. Bananas, coconuts, persimmons and other tropical fruit also thrive in this climate.

The average temperature in the lowlands is about 86 degrees. The sun is blazing hot and Nicaraguans often try to protect themselves from its damaging effects. Women carry umbrellas to provide some shade if they are out in the open for a long time. Men wear straw hats with strings that are tied into a knot under the chin to shade their eyes while working in the fields or walking outside.

Very few homes have air conditioning. Many people do not have electric fans. In Managua, a few upper-class homes, offices and restaurants have air conditioning. Most people have to tolerate the heat. Young Nicaraguans faithfully followed fashion fads, even when it meant wearing clothes made of plastic, a style that was a popular one in the discos in the mid 1980s.

Major cities are Managua, Grenada and Leon. Managua became an important city in 1852 when two rival political factions, the Liberals and the Conservatives settled their differences by choosing the sleepy town as the nation's capital. Before this decision, Leon and Granada were the two most important cities in Nicaragua. The Liberals dominated Leon and the Conservatives controlled Granada. The two groups fought many battles before agreeing to make Managua the capital. Managua is close to a major fault line near a volcano where earthquakes occur frequently. In 1972, a severe earthquake killed 10,000 people in Managua and the city was destroyed. Recovery of Managua has been a slow process. Parts of Managua still lie in ruins and future earthquakes have hindered plans to rebuild the city. Development in Managua has been outside the city where new neighborhoods, shops and restaurants are being built. Over the past decade, a few modern shopping malls with department stores and movie theaters have sprung up in Managua, along with numerous modern supermarkets and American fast food restaurants.

GRANADA is Nicaragua's oldest city and it was founded in 1524 by Spanish explorer Francisco Hernandez de Cordoba. Like Managua, it is also located on the shore of a lake and near a volcano. It is Nicaragua's second largest city. It is an important commercial area. Grenada's volcano has left the area around the town fertile and coffee and sugarcane are two important crops grown there. Granada has seen its share of fighting caused by political conflict, which has ravaged the country for years. Many factories and buildings have suffered heavy damage and are still being repaired. There are a hundred or so tiny islands east of Granada in Lake Nicaragua. These isletas are said to have been created when Granada's volcano erupted, blowing its lake-facing side into the water. The islands are linked by motorboat taxis and wealthy Nicaraguans have built cottages there for weekend retreats.

LEON was founded by Hernandez. In the Spanish colonial period, it was the capital of Nicaragua. Leon has a huge cathedral which looks like a cathedral in Lima, the capital of Peru, another Spanish colony. Outside the city are beaches, resort towns and a fertile agricultural area. Much of the dry, flat plain around the city is planted with cotton.

Almost half of the employed people in Nicaragua work on farms. During the dry season, when crops are harvested, schools are closed so that children can help with the farm work. Many crops such as beans, bananas, sugarcane and rice grow well in Nicaraguan soil. Corn, coffee, cotton, tobacco and cacao are the most important crops while beans and rice are grown mainly for domestic consumption. Nicaragua's chief agricultural exports are coffee, beef, sugar and seafood. Gold, silver, copper, tungsten, lead and zinc are important resources. Timber is another natural resource. Valuable mahogany, ebony and rosewood trees grow in the highlands and the northern Atlantic area is rich in pines.

About 16 percent of the land in Nicaragua or 8,000 square miles of the land is suitable for growing things. Of this land, roughly 1,000 square miles are actively cultivated. Another large portion of the land is used for grazing cattle.

Many varieties of plants and animals are indigenous to Nicaragua and other Central American countries. Some of these plants and trees are cedar, oak and pine trees. Tropical plants are tamarind and persimmon trees.

Many animal species found in North America also live in Nicaragua. Deer, rattlesnakes and coyotes are common in the highlands and in some sections of the western lowlands. There are toucans, sleuths, monkeys, jaguars, wild boars and boa constrictors. Coral reefs are also found off the coast.

Aztecs and Maya of Mexico lived in Nicaragua about 600 to 1,000 years ago. The Nicaraos inhabited much of the Pacific lowlands. Corn and beans were their main crops. Indigenous people hunted for fish and practiced slash-and-burn agriculture. Their staple foods were root crops such as cassava, plantains and pineapples. The Nicarao people produced beautiful works of art such as pottery and gold jewelry. Religion and trading were important to their lives.

Nicaragua declared independence from Spain in 1821. It became part of the Mexican Empire. In 1823 Nicaragua left the Mexican Empire to join the United Provinces of Central America. In 1838 Nicaragua became an independent republic. In 1856 William Walker, an American adventurer, became president of Nicaragua. He sold or gave land to U.S. companies and declared English the official language. He tried to make Nicaragua part of the United States.

Nicaragua's two warring parties joined forces and recruited many peasants to help fight William Walker. The people of Nicaragua succeeded in overthrowing Walker and forced him to leave the country. However, from 1857 to 1893 almost all the presidents were conservatives. They had passed laws that made it harder for peasants to own land, essentially taking away the farmers' livelihood. By 1900, distinct class boundaries had formed, dividing poor peasant farmers from the wealthy landowners for whom they worked.

Four hundred U.S. Marines were sent to Nicaragua to preserve order when Zelaya was president in 1893. Many Nicaraguans, especially conservatives, opposed Zelaya, a harsh dictator. When Zelaya resigned in 1909, another person, Jose Madriz, took Zelaya's place. The civil war in Nicaragua continued for several more months until conservative president Adolfo Diaz took office in 1911.

Diaz made an agreement that turned over control of the country's finances to the United States of America until 1925 when debts were paid off.

From 1927 to 1933 General Augusto Cesar Sandino was the leader. He organized Sandinista and adopted guerilla tactics, with small groups hiding in the mountains and periodically ambushing to attack the U.S. Marines. In 1934 after the U.S. Marines left Nicaragua, President Sacasa and General Sandino signed a peace treaty to end the fighting. In 1936 General Somoza forced President Sacasa to resign. Somoza became the next president of Nicaragua. Somoza had absolute power over the country's activities and used it to his personal advantage. In the 1940s the United States persuaded Somoza not to run for another term. Somoza then appointed a family friend to the presidency. In 1950 Somoza then assumed the presidency. Somoza was shot in 1956 so that his dictatorship was ended. Somoza's eldest son Luis took over. When Luis died his younger brother, Anastasio took over this country and ruled by his father's methods. He increased his family wealth to 900 million. The Somoza family owned one-fifth of the country's land, several sugar mills, factories, an airline and several banks.

The Sandinistas ruled Nicaragua from 1979 to 1990. They tried to help the poor and improve the economy. A new civil war hampered the Sandinistas' efforts at social reform. By the early 1980s a new group of rebels had formed. They were called Contras. By 1981 the U.S. government thought the Sandinistas were communists who would allow the Soviet Union to set up military bases in Nicaragua. In 1985, Ronald Reagan, President of the U.S.A., authorized military aid to the Contras and in 1985 declared a trade embargo on Nicaragua. In 1990 Violeta de Barrios Chamarro, the first female president was endorsed by the United States because she planned to establish democracy in Nicaragua and introduce a market economy. Chamarro initiated the creation of democratic institutions, worked toward national reconciliation, stabilized the economy and reduced human rights violations. Dona Violeta, as Nicaraguans call her, became a beloved national figure. In 2001 Aleman's former vice president, Enrique Balanos, was elected president. Balanos promised to address poverty, unemployment and corruption and also to seek relief from the country's burden of international debt. In 2004, Nicaragua's national debt was forgiven by 80 percent by the World Bank.

COSTA RICA

Costa Rica is in Central America. It is a little smaller than West Virginia. Mountains cover much of Costa Rica. San Jose is the capital of Costa Rica. Nicaragua is north of Costa Rica and Panama is southeast of Costa Rica. A central mountain plateau has rich soil and a cool climate. The Pacific coast is rocky. Te Caribbean coast is hot and rainy. Forests along the coasts have more than 100 kinds of trees.

Coffee plants grow well on the slopes of the Monteverde Cloud Forest. In the past, forests covered most of Costa Rica. But people cut down many forests for farmland. Now, Costa Rica protects its forests and wild life. Many birds, snakes, frogs, monkeys and other animals live in 23 national parks.

Costa Rica became a colony of Spain in the 1500s. When the Spanish tried to force Costa Rican Indians to work for them, they escaped from the Spanish into the forests. In the early 1800s, the Spanish colony of Mexico fought for its freedom from Spain. In 1821, Mexico declared its independence from Spain. It formed an empire that included Costa Rica.

Agustin Iturbide became the emperor. The empire broke up in 1823. Costa Rica then became an independent country.

Costa Rica's government is a democratic republic. Every four years, Costa Ricans age 18 and older must vote. The people vote for a president and two vice presidents. The president is the head of the government. The people also vote for members of the Legislative Assembly. The Assembly makes the country's laws. It is similar to the U.S. Congress. The Assembly meets in the National Palace in San Jose, the capital city.

Most Costa Ricans live in houses. City houses have cement block walls and iron roofs. Rural houses have either cement or wood walls. Most rural houses have a front porch where families can sit together and talk with neighbors. Costa Ricans often paint their houses bright pink, green or blue. 60 percent of the people live in the urban area. 40 percent of Costa Ricans live in the rural area.

Costa Rica does not have enough housing for everyone. Many large cities such as San Jose, Miramar, San Isidro, Nicoya, Santa Cruz, Liberia, Tilaran, Alajuela, Puerto Limon, etc. are crowded and do not have enough housing. Some people build houses with old wood and iron. Many houses do not have water or electricity. The people in such neighborhoods are quite poor.

Costa Rica has many kinds of transportation such as cars, trucks, and buses which go down narrow city streets. Streets in large cities such as San Jose are often filled with long lines of cars and buses. Many people take a bus to work.

Most people also travel by bus between towns. In the mountains the roads are mostly dirt. In some areas, people still ride horses from place to place. Much of the Caribbean coast is swampy. The government dug a canal to connect the port cities. Water taxis carry people through the wetlands. Farmers take bananas and other tropical fruit on motorboats.

Most people in Costa Rica work in service industries such as schools, government offices and hospitals. Costa Rica's national parks attract many visitors every year. Costa Ricans work in parks, hotels and restaurants.

In the rural areas, most people are farmers. They grow coffee, bananas, sugarcane and pineapples. Many bananas sold in the United States come from Costa Rica. Ranchers in the northwest raise cattle. Other Costa Ricans work in factories. Many prepare food or sew clothing. A large computer chip company built a factory in Costa Rica in 1998. Computer factories provide many new jobs. Workers on banana plantations sort bananas with the help of machines.

School is free for all children from grade school through high school. Children between ages 7 and 13 must go to school. The school year lasts from March to November. In cities, classes in public schools are large. Some parents pay for their children to go to private schools. In the rural areas, many students go to a one-room schoolhouse. Students of all ages study together.

Some rural schools only have a few books. Teachers must make copies of the books for their students.

Soccer is Costa Rica's favorite sport. Every small town has a soccer field. People get very excited when they watch their favorite team. If their team wins, fans honk their car horns.

Good beaches line both coasts. Surfing in the Pacific Ocean is a popular sport. Surfing became popular in the 1990s. Some surfers live on the Pacific coast beaches. They surf the biggest waves in the morning.

Costa Rica's national symbol is a painted ox cart .In the past, farmers filled the carts with coffee beans. Oxen pulled the carts to market. Bright red, orange and yellow designs covered the carts. Today, artists still paint small ox carts for parades and for tourists. Painting ox carts is a tradition that is more than one hundred years old.

In northwest Costa Rica, the descendants of the Chorotega Indians make pottery by hand. These artists respect nature. They paint lizards, bats or jaguars on their pots. The otters teach their children to make pottery. They also teach the grade-school children in their villages.

Every town in Costa Rica holds a festival every year. Sometimes the festivals honor Catholic saints. Other festivals raise money for a church school or hospital. Many festivals include giant masked clowns. People enjoy games, parades and music. Costa Ricans celebrate

Easter, Independence, Labor Day, Mothers' Day and New Year's Day.

Most Costa Ricans celebrate the Roman Catholic holidays. For Christmas, families decorate their homes with colored lights. The children write to the Christ child to ask for presents. Families set up tall statues of Mary, Joseph and baby Jesus.

Costa Ricans celebrate Independence Day on September 15. Children all over Costa Rica dress up and take part in parades. To celebrate Independence Day, girls dress in costumes for a parade. Their sashes tell which town they come from.

Most Costa Ricans eat black beans and rice with every meal. The traditional breakfast of rice and beans is called gallo pinto. Sometimes eggs, tortillas and sour cream are added. Other meals include beef or chicken with rice and beans.

In most cities, Costa Ricans sell sweets from a street stand. Coconut cakes, fudge and roasted bananas are popular snacks. Many people like cold drinks made from bananas, pineapples or strawberries. The fruit is mixed with ice and milk.

In the past, people stayed in their home villages. Now, young people move to the cities for good jobs. On Sundays and holidays, people return to their home village. They go to parks or visit with their families.

Natural resources in Costa Rica are fisheries, forests and hydroelectric power. 76% of the people are Roman Catholics. 16% are Protestants and 8% other religions.

Costa Rica's money is the colon. In 2005, one U.S. dollar equaled 465 colones. The Costa Rican flag has five stripes. The coat of arms is the red stripe. The seven stars in the coat of arms represent Costa Rica's seven provinces.

Costa Rica is one of the most interesting and beautiful places to visit as a tourist in Central America because of its scenic beaches, verdant jungles and forests and friendly people.

Costa Rica is the only nation in Central and South America that has not had a war since its independence. For over 150 years it is the only nation in Latin America where tourists have been able to visit without worrying about risking a war, revolution and terrorists. It has become one of the most popular, tropical, tourist destinations in the world.

PANAMA

The Isthmus of Panama, the Republic of Panama, acted as a land bridge between the Americas, providing animals and people with a route of biological and cultural exchange. When Europeans arrived, the isthmus took on a new identity. It became a barricade blocking European traders from their ultimate goals which were Asian trading ports of the Orient. The isthmus turned out to be a gold mine. The Spanish lived in Panama and stripped its people and countryside of its wealth. For nearly three hundred years, Panama remained a Spanish settlement whose resources and people were exploited.

The Panama of today has survived and it has emerged as a rich, culturally diverse place. It has a thriving business section in which the nations of the world come to trade. It is a crossroads for ships traveling from the Pacific to the Atlantic and a passageway from North to South America. It is a tourist spot where international travelers come to enjoy some of nature's most beautiful places in the world.

Panama means "abundance of fish." Today, it also means an abundance of culture, history and peoples. However, centuries of strife, war, devastation, conquest and exploration pervade all aspects of Panamanian life. Panama is still healing from the attempts by a dictator. Slowly, however, Panamanians have gained a voice by becoming a democratic nation.

The nineteenth century General Simon Bolivar once said, "If the world had to choose a capital, the Isthmus of Panama would be the obvious place for that high destiny." Panama Province is home to nearly half of the country's population---a population that is quite diversified. There are Spanish, African, West Indian, Chinese, Indian, European and North Americans that make a compelling cultural mix, creating perhaps the most outward looking society in Central America.

All that remains of the city of Old Panama are stone ruins. The pirate, Henry Morgan burned the whole town to the ground in 1671. After that, the city was moved west a few miles. The center of the city has moved farther west to the Panama Canal. In Punta Paitilla, skyscrapers and modern city streets make up the bustling business district. Just northwest of here is the Metropolitan Natural Park, a 655 acre park within the city containing a large piece of land made up of a specific kind of natural habitat known as the Lowland Pacific Forest, which is home to 45 mammals, 36 reptiles, 14 amphibian and 227 bird species.

Panama City is the national capital of Panama. El Valle is a popular tourist spot for visitors to Panama because of the cool climate and fertile soil formation. The farmers of El Valle are able to grow delicate fruits and vegetables that are difficult to maintain in the hotter climates below, such as tomatoes and strawberries. El Valle is home to many delicate wild, flowers including orchids. El Valle is most famous for producing a white orchid called the holy ghost, Panama's national flower. Other attractions in El Valle are thermal baths that are heated from hot springs near the Anton River. There are odd looking "Square Trees", named because their trunks do not grow round but instead have fur flat sides. There are also golden frogs which have become the unofficial mascots of El Valle. A popular activity in El Valle is to go looking for these one inch long, yellow, black-spotted frogs in the rain forests surrounding towns.

The Panama Canal is located in the province of Panama. People from all over the world come to see the Panama Canal. Work began on the Panama Canal in 1881. William Crawford Gorgas went to Panama in 1904 to build the Panama Canal. The United States leased a six mile wide strip stretching from Colon to Panama City. The United States had control over all the parts, the canal, the railroad and its own courts within this area. President Theodore Roosevelt recognized the new Panamanian government. Phillipe Bunou-Varilla, acting as the Panamanian representative to the United States, signed the Ha-Bunou Varilla Treaty with John Hay, the U.S. secretary of state. This transferred the concessions of the Hay-Herron Treaty from Columbia to Panama. Because of the treaty, the Republic of Panama came under the protection of the United States on February 23, 1904. The treaty also gave the United States the power to intervene in Panama's domestic affairs if the canal was threatened.

The Panama Canal was a gigantic architectural undertaking unlike any other in history. $352,000,000 was spent on the Panama Canal. French and American expenditures came to $639,000,000. Many workers died because of mosquitoes which caused yellow fever. After nearly thirty-four years of construction, the Panama Canal was opened to its first seafaring vessel, the Ancon, on August 15, 1914, which passed through without a hitch.

Some 13 to 14 thousand vessels use the Canal every year. Commercial transportation activities through the Canal represent approximately 5% of the world trade. The Canal has a work force of approximately 9 thousand employees and operates 24 hours a day, 365 days a year, providing transit service to vessels of all nations without discrimination.

General Omar Torrijos Herrera wielded enormous political power in Panama. He signed a treaty with the United States in 1977 giving Panama authority over the Canal Zone. In 1972 Omar Torrijos supported the formation of the 505 member National Assembly of Municipal Representatives that voted to confirm his role as the leader of Panama. The assembly ratified the first of Panama's new constitution, greatly enhancing Omar Torrijos Herrera's power.

Later, Manuel Antonio Noriega rose to the position of commander in chief just before the 1984 elections were held. The United States decided to forcefully eliminate Noriega from Panama. Noriega surrendered to U.S. forces in January 1990 and was later taken to the United states to stand trial for his crimes.

In 1994, the first fully democratic election since 1948, Ernesto Perez Balladores, a Panamanian businessman, won the presidency. Later on, in 1999 elections Mireya Moscaso, the widow of Arnulfo Arias, was elected president under the Arnulfista Party. On December 31 of that year, she saw her husband's dream of attaining Panamanian sovereignty over the canal come true. Finally Panama was truly independent.

Agriculture is a large industry in Panama. Some popular crops are bananas, shrimp and coffee. Other crops include rice, corn, sugarcane, vegetables and livestock. The main exports are bananas, shrimp and coffee. These exports are shipped mainly to the United States of America. Panama also imports a lot of supplies from the United States.

One way Panama hopes to grow as a country is through international trade. The United States of America is Panama's biggest investment and trading partner. Free-trade agreements will help Panama grow.

The people of Panama are a diverse mix of nationalities, cultural practices, languages and customs. Panama's diversity of people is due in large part to its role as a crossroads, between the Americas and the Pacific and Atlantic oceans. International trading in Panama's ports brought in by the Panama Canal has drawn in a wide range of people who now call Panama their home. The people are Chinese, Jews, Arabs, Greeks, South Asians, Lebanese, Western Europeans and North Americans. Whites and culturally integrated Indians are grouped into the mestizo population. The word mestizo simply means a person of mixed racial ancestry. The mestizo population of Panama is largely made up of people of mixed European, mainly Spanish and American Indian blood.

Roman Catholicism is the largest religion in Panama. 82 percent of Panamanians identify themselves as Roman Catholic. Roman Catholicism was the official religion of Spain when Spanish settlers populated Panama in the 1500s and Catholicism has remained the predominant religion ever since. The next largest religious group in Panama, Protestants make up about ten percent of the population. Many other religions are practiced throughout Panama as well. Mormons number thirty-four thousand people. There are also Seventh-Day Adventists and Episcopalians. Jehovah's Witnesses have around ten thousand members. The Jewish community, concentrated largely in Panama City, is made up of a generally wealthier economic section of the population and accounts for more than seven thousand people. Muslims living in Panama number around five thousand and live mostly in Colon.

Antillean Blacks or West Indian blacks come from Jamaica, Haiti and Puerto Rico. Black laborers from the British West Indies came to Panama by the tens of thousands in the first half of the twentieth century. Most of them were involved in the effort to improve the isthmus transportation system. Many came to work in the country's banana plantations. By 1910, the Panama Canal Company had employed more than 50,000 workers. Three-quarters of them were Antillean blacks. They formed the nucleus of a community separated from the larger society by race, language, religion and culture.

The indigenous peoples of Panama make up approximately six percent of the population. They can be divided into six major tribes. The indigenous tribes of Panama are the Kuna, the Guaymi, the Embera, the Woumaan, the Teribe and the Bokota. Because of their cultural similarities and the fact that they live close to each other, the Embers and the Woumaan are usually grouped together as are the Teribe and the Bokota. The indigenous cultures of Panama have been struggling for nearly five hundred years ever since the first Spanish explorers arrived.

The Kuna tribe lives in the dense tropical rain forest and their isolation has helped preserve their traditional culture. The Kuna are the oldest present-day inhabitants of the isthmus around ten thousand years ago. Their culture has been largely protected from outside influences by surrounding swamps, dense tropical rain forest and the San Blas range to the south. As a result, their language, customs and genetics remain the purest examples of an indigenous population in Panama.

The society of the Kuna is matriarchal, which means that inheritances pass through the women instead of the men. Upon marrying, young men must move into the house of their mother-in-law. Daughters are prized over sons because of their ability to produce children. Labor is divided by gender. A husband gathers coconuts, performs repairs on the house, collects firewood and makes clothes for his sons. Wives prepare food, clean the house, gather fresh water, unload boats and make clothes for the women of the family. Kuna women have retained their traditional dress much more than the men have and their clothing is often a spectacular array of vibrant colors.

Tourism has affected indigenous people of Panama. Tourists have brought an influx of Western-style goods and clothes. Guaymi Indians play traditional games and a variety of musical instruments during their festivals. Guaymi music is performed at festivals. Members of the Guaymi tribe are very musical and play a variety of instruments such as the conch shell, called a dru and a mouth harp known as a truma. The talero is a flutelike instrument which is used to call gatherings and to welcome friends. At these festivals a number of traditional games are played. Traditional dances are performed.

The Embera tribe has around 15,000 inhabitants. They are often grouped with the Wounaan tribe. Both these groups may have migrated northwest sometime between the 1600s and 1700s from the Chaco region of Columbia. Both tribes may have been in Panama before the Spaniards arrived there.

The Teribe live in twenty-seven communities in Bocas Del Taro Province. The Teribe tribe subsist mainly through its agriculture, growing platanos, corn, coffee, cocoa, jobo, guanabana, pineapple, guayaha, oranges and lemons. They also raise chickens and turkeys. Hunting is done with bows and arrows and sometimes rifles to kill rabbits, etc. The Teribe add to their income by making hammocks and baskets to sell.

The Bribri tribe from Costa Rican Talamanca tribe crossed the Costa Rican border sometime during the twentieth century to find work on Panamanian banana plantations. Only about five hundred Bribri people live in Panama today.

Panama continues to expand its role as an international crossroads and area of trade. Panama's future depends on its expansion and economic growth. Democracy has strengthened Panama and brought more stability to the people of Panama. Tourism continues to grow and expand in Panama.